if you 're

clueless

about

Starting

Your Own

Business

and

want to

know more

by SETH GODIN

DEARBORN™
A **Kaplan Professional** Company

If You're Clueless about Starting Your Own Business and Want to Know More

Associate Publisher: Cynthia A. Zigmund
Senior Managing Editor: Jack Kiburz
Interior and Cover Design: Karen Engelmann

© 1998 by Seth Godin Productions, Inc.

Published by Dearborn, a Kaplan Professional Company

Printed in the United States of America

10 9 8 7 6 5

Library of Congress Cataloging-in-Publication Data
Godin, Seth.
    If you're clueless about starting your own business and want to
  know more / by Seth Godin.
        p.   cm.
    Includes bibliographical references and index.
    ISBN 1-57410-093-9
    1. New business enterprises.   2. Success in business   I. Title.
  HD62.5.G633 1997
  658'.041--dc21   97-26369
                                                                CIP

Dearborn books are available at special quantity discounts to use as premiums and sales promotions, or for use in corporate training programs. For more information, please call the Special Sales Manager at 800-621-9621, ext. 4514, or write to Dearborn Financial Publishing, Inc., 155 North Wacker Drive, Chicago, IL 60606-1719.

Acknowledgments

Thanks to Jack Kiburz and Cindy Zigmund at Dearborn whose editorial guidance made this book possible. Karen Watts was the driving force behind the Clueless concept, and Mark Henricks did an expert job of pulling it all together.

Thanks to Robin Dellabough, Lisa DiMona, Nana Sledzieski, Ann Weinerman, Emily Gold, Rachel Sussman, Susan Kushnick, Lisa Lindsay, Julie Maner, and Sarah Silbert at SGP for their never-ending insight and hard work. And kudos to Sidney Short for his layout work, Theresa Casaboon for her copyediting talent, and Suzanne Herel for her expert proofreading.

Contents

This Time It's Personal

If you've read any of the other books in the Clueless series, you've learned a lot about the stock market, insurance, or investments. Those books will make your life easier, help you save money, or even make you wealthy. But this book is different. It's personal. It's about a decision that will change virtually every aspect of your life.

Starting your own business is the American dream. Every year, thousands of people take the plunge. And when they do, they discover the rewards, the risks, and the pitfalls that entrepreneurs face. It's not like anything else you'll ever do, and it can be so rewarding, so challenging, and so engaging that you won't be able to imagine ever doing anything else.

In this book, I'm going to try to share with you some of the lessons I've learned from starting and running several businesses. I've been the sole proprietor of a home-based business, running around in my pajamas, as well as the CEO of a venture-backed Internet start-up company, complete with the suit and tie. Along the way, I've discovered three things:

1. You're the only one in charge.

2. Resilience and persistence are the two most important attributes you'll need.

3. Being prepared makes a big difference.

There are no schools for entrepreneurs. No licenses needed. No inspectors, no supervisors, no bosses. Entrepreneurs set their own agendas, choose their own courses. That freedom and responsibility is an elixir for some, poison for others. Hopefully, this book will help you discover (before you go too far) whether this lifestyle is for you by giving you a heads up about the planning you'll need, the decisions you'll be facing, the kinds of issues you'll have to wrestle with.

The day I decided to run my own business was one of the most important I can remember. Every day since then, I've learned more, taught more, and had more fun than I could ever imagine having in a "real" job. Welcome to the world of the entrepreneur. And good luck!

GETTING a clue about starting a small BUSINESS

Do you day-dream about starting your own business? Are you the talented employee who believes she could **do better** for herself as the boss? Are you the guy who has done well for others but is ready to try something new for himself?

If your answer is, "Yes…but I don't think I could ever actually do that," think again. Because we're not talking about the lottery or some other remote pipe dream. We're talking about the American Dream. If you're reading this book, then you've already taken the first successful step towards starting your business. Now keep going!

The prospect of self-reliance and financial freedom has driven thousands of people toward starting and building a business that provides rewards a regular job just can't. But the challenges of starting and building your own business far outweigh the day-to-day demands you face working for someone else.

1

LEARN FROM A GURU

Believe it or not, you rarely have to start a new business from scratch. The number of businesses that are based on 100 percent brand-new ideas is pretty small.

Once you decide what sort of business you'd like to run, find someone who's already doing it successfully. She might be in a different city, or servicing a different market. Then learn all you can from this guru. Discover the best techniques, the best software, the best systems, everything. You'll be amazed at how much people will tell you if you ask them.

Keep your eyes open for potential gurus in trade magazines that cover your industry. Once you find one, write a letter asking her for a 20-minute phone call. When you get her on the phone, ask two pointed questions that show you understand your business and are eager to learn. Chances are she'll be flattered that you asked and eager to help.

There are no rules. No safety nets. No manuals. You're very much on your own, holding the double-edged sword of freedom. When you run your own business, the customer, the marketplace, and your suppliers all become your new bosses. If you found that pleasing one boss was a hassle, you're in for a surprise.

The reality is that entrepreneurship is a tremendously exhilarating route for some people, and an extremely frustrating and defeating experience for many others. But getting a clue means understanding that there are steps you can take right from the start that will give you an edge. You have to assess your skills and experience, measure your level of enthusiasm, and prepare and execute your well-thought-out plan. People with plans are less likely to quit. And as an entrepreneur, if you don't quit, you win.

It's Really All About You

Starting a business is a big commitment. It changes your financial picture, your lifestyle, and in all probability, your relationships, both personal and professional. Taking a hard look at why you're doing it and what you expect from it is worth the time—it's a lot easier to change course now than it will be later.

The first thing you need to do is assess your own strengths and weaknesses. Explore your motivations and discover whether or not you have what it takes to make it all happen. Are you ready and

What Business Are You In, Anyway?

Whatever business you think you're in—manufacturing, retailing, restaurant, service—the only business you're really in is sales. From the very beginning, no matter what you produce, you'll be selling that product—first to potential backers to get them to invest the money, next to your employees to get them excited about it, and eventually to your customers to get them to buy it. So whatever you consider your strengths, whatever you perceive as your skills and talents, think of yourself primarily as a salesperson.

It's easy for a new entrepreneur to focus on the "factory," to be sure that the soup tastes great, that the shipping boxes are ready, that all the paperwork is perfect. These details are important, but the fact is, businesses never succeed because of any them. They succeed if people want to buy what they have to sell.

As you think about starting your business, a big question to ask yourself is, "Is someone going to pay for my product or service?" And the second question is, "How can I communicate what I sell to my potential customers so that they will buy it?"

If you're a freelancer, however, you do need to pay attention to the factory. Why? Because you *are* the factory, and your ability to make things better than everyone else is critically important.

BEND WITH THE WIND

Rigidity is the enemy of the successful entrepreneur. The ability to change with the market and to adapt to new conditions is critical.

Remember Western Union? It was one of the greatest, most profitable companies in our history—a giant in the communications industry. Today, all that remains is the brand name and a small cash transfer service. Western Union could have become Federal Express. It had the money, the brand name, and the access to launch what would have become a billion-dollar business. But it was rigid. It stuck with a dying business, and now it's a small speck on the radar screen.

The same thing can happen to the local sandwich shop, the typesetting guy down the corner, or the entrepreneur building a new piece of software. Understanding the changing market and not being too proud to acknowledge it is a critical step in your journey.

willing to expend a huge amount of energy to accomplish your goals? Do you know what traits are common to successful business people? Do you have those traits?

This book will take you on a series of self-exploratory expeditions to discover the answers to these questions. Start by taking the "Entrepreneurial Personality Test" on page eight. Then, use chapter two to evaluate if you've got the skills and experience. Even if you've never started a business, you probably already have a vast supply of resources that you can call upon—maybe even more than you think. You don't need special training to be a successful entrepreneur—but you do need basic skills that will increase your chances of success.

Chapter three will help you set the goals you need to stay focused as you go about the process of getting started and building your business. A businessperson with written goals is far more likely to succeed than one without them—and this book will lay the foundation you need to set those goals.

Before you get down to the particulars of running a business, you'll want to give serious thought to how to position your business to make the most of the market (chapter four), and also to make some simple decisions about the optimum way to set up your business in the eyes of the law (chapter five). These two decisions will shape the content and structure of your business, and the time you invest in them now will pay big dividends later on.

There Are Two—Okay, Three—Kinds of Small Businesses

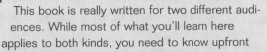

This book is really written for two different audiences. While most of what you'll learn here applies to both kinds, you need to know upfront which path you're on. It will save you a lot of heartache and confusion. You can choose to be a freelancer (which is what most small businesspeople are) or you can be an entrepreneur.

An entrepreneur works to build a business bigger than herself, with significant financial risks and numerous employees. A freelancer, on the other hand, is looking for the freedom and profit that come from being on your own, without the headaches that come from building a significant venture.

If you're interested in a better lifestyle, control over your time, and not too much risk, you're a freelancer. You call the shots, you work for people who need you, and you'll view your business as a series of engagements with clients. That doesn't mean you have to work out of an attic. If you own a small bookstore with an employee or three and no dreams of beating Barnes & Noble, you're a freelancer. If you want to have a small ad agency with a few clients and some great ads, you're a freelancer. Why? Because your product is you. You've found yourself a great job, with more control than most employees and a lot more hassle!

On the other hand, if you're on a mission, if you're looking to build an organization, become wealthy, or just grow something bigger than yourself, you're on track to be an entrepreneur.

Buying a franchise fits into a third category—one that's sort of a blend of the first two. This book doesn't focus on the franchise route, as it is so different from most of what a traditional small businessperson does. However, keeping the three straight will make your choices a whole lot easier!

The most successful entrepreneurs have a plan and in chapter six, you'll build one. Actually, you'll build several, all of which will help you think about the big picture in terms of smaller tasks that are easier to manage. They'll also help you secure financial backers (the folks who will be lending you start-up cash) if you need them.

The remainder of this book will lead you through the steps of actually obtaining any financing you may seek (chapter seven), getting the doors open (chapter eight), and spreading the word to your most valuable asset: the customers (chapter nine).

Eventually the time will come when you may want to hire more help, add new products, or venture into other markets. Chapter ten will provide the information you need. Don't forget to check out the resources section, where you'll find other books, newsletters, organizations, and online sources that will keep you informed about all the finer details of running your business.

Do You Have the Entrepreneurial Personality?

It's a myth that there's one entrepreneurial type. Bill Gates is an entrepreneur, but so is the single mom who runs a typing service out of her home. While the media has glamorized the macho, take-no-prisoners approach to growing businesses into billion-dollar companies, the fact is that most jobs are created by the tiny "mom-and-pop" start-ups that are everywhere. You're far more likely to start and run a successful two- or three-person company than you are to raise venture capital and go public.

That said, there are several traits that successful entrepreneurs have in common. If you've got them, great! If not, it may be worth taking another look at whether this path is for you. The single most important thing you need to succeed in business is a positive, committed attitude. Almost all small businesses fail sooner or later, and those that don't are buffeted by change, insecurity, and indecision. If you're likely to give up in the face of this sort of challenge, save your money and keep your day job. If there's one thing successful entrepreneurs have in common, it's resilience.

Entrepreneurs enjoy a challenge, are able to handle a lot of stress, and are organized, yet flexible. If you haven't guessed it already, you also need to work at a tremendously high energy level for long periods of time. It takes courage and determination, and a

Does This Sound Familiar?

Do you recognize yourself at all in any of these profiles?

These are all people who should take the plunge and start their own businesses. If you're anything like them, you should, too.

• The middle manager who believes he can go out and make it on his own

• The career-changer who is going to open a pet store because she loves dogs

• The restaurant chef who is going to open up his own restaurant

• The graphic designer going out on her own

• The accountant leaving a big firm to start his own tax service

• The sales rep who wants to choose his own products

• The retiree who wants to buy a small store

• The book editor who wants to become a literary agent

• The lawyer with three friends ready to form a partnership

• The technology maven with a great idea

willingness to take responsibility for yourself. And if you've got employees, you're responsible for other people as well.

Entrepreneurs are usually more comfortable being in charge than following directions. They enjoy pulling projects together and naturally take the initiative to lead other people. They are passionate about their vision and firmly believe that there are substantial financial and emotional rewards that go with it. That's important to remember, because launching a business requires a sense of excitement and urgency that must be passed along to your investors, your employees, and your customers.

One of the most difficult aspects of building your own business is making it through the inevitable "tough times." According to Joseph R. Mancuso, founder of the Center for Entrepreneurial Management, the world's largest nonprofit association of entrepreneurial managers, the failure rate among new businesses is over 50 percent in the first two years of operation. Over 90 percent don't make it to their tenth birthday. That's not meant to discourage you; it merely demonstrates the reality of some of the tough times you may face: competitors appear from nowhere, potential clients are reluctant to try new products, managing employees and their personalities becomes a whole separate career, and the government adds its own set of burdens in the form of regulations and taxes. Determination and perseverance will give you the strength to keep pushing forward despite the obstacles.

The ability to sell yourself and your business is another key element in entrepreneurial success. Don't fool yourself—sooner or later, it's all about bringing money in the door. Spike Lee sells himself to movie studios who finance his films. The graphic designer who starts his own studio needs to cold call clients and sell them as well. If you don't have the stomach and the confidence to do this, if you believe that the world will beat a path to your door, you need to take a hard look at what sort of business you're considering.

The Test

Take this "Entrepreneurial Personality Test"* to get a sense of how well suited you are to the entrepreneurial lifestyle. Answer the questions quickly, without analyzing what you think the "right" answer might be.

1. I generally try to take charge of things when I am with people.
   a. Strongly agree
   b. Moderately agree
   c. Moderately disagree
   d. Strongly disagree

2. I am acutely aware of the passage of time and often press myself to complete a task.
   a. Strongly agree
   b. Moderately agree
   c. Moderately disagree
   d. Strongly disagree

3. I dislike taking orders from others or being told what to do.
   a. Strongly agree
   b. Moderately agree
   c. Moderately disagree
   d. Strongly disagree

4. I would want my employees to be content, but not at the expense of my business.
   a. Strongly agree
   b. Moderately agree
   c. Moderately disagree
   d. Strongly disagree

5. Given reasonable odds, my efforts can successfully influence the outcome.
   a. Strongly agree
   b. Moderately agree
   c. Moderately disagree
   d. Strongly disagree

6. Things that typically unnerve most people do not ruffle me.
   a. Strongly agree
   b. Moderately agree
   c. Moderately disagree
   d. Strongly disagree

7. I seem to have a much higher energy level than most people.
   a. Strongly agree
   b. Moderately agree
   c. Moderately disagree
   d. Strongly disagree

8. I believe that there is a proper time for everything, and things can't be rushed.
   a. Strongly agree
   b. Moderately agree
   c. Moderately disagree
   d. Strongly disagree

9. I have often been in the position of directing or leading projects or groups.
   a. Strongly agree
   b. Moderately agree
   c. Moderately disagree
   d. Strongly disagree

10. When confronted with a complex task, I am generally able to pull it all together myself—and in fact enjoy doing so.
    a. Strongly agree
    b. Moderately agree
    c. Moderately disagree
    d. Strongly disagree

11. Even if I disliked doing it, I would be able to fire an employee who was not productive.
    a. Strongly agree
    b. Moderately agree
    c. Moderately disagree
    d. Strongly disagree

*Reprinted with the permission of Simon & Schuster from *The Field Guide to Starting a Business* by Mark Levine and Stephen M. Pollan. Copyright © 1990 by Mark Levine and Stephen M. Pollan.

12. Once I've launched a venture, I find it difficult to change my course, even if the prospects of success are exceedingly dim.
    a. Strongly agree   c. Moderately disagree
    b. Moderately agree   d. Strongly disagree

13. I would readily leave a well-paying, high-status job to start my own business, even if it meant tightening my belt considerably for a while.
    a. Strongly agree   c. Moderately disagree
    b. Moderately agree   d. Strongly disagree

14. I can do just about anything I set my mind to do.
    a. Strongly agree   c. Moderately disagree
    b. Moderately agree   d. Strongly disagree

15. Others say I have a sharp, analytical mind.
    a. Strongly agree   c. Moderately disagree
    b. Moderately agree   d. Strongly disagree

16. I have worked long, hard hours for long periods of time, and I would do so again if necessary.
    a. Strongly agree   c. Moderately disagree
    b. Moderately agree   d. Strongly disagree

17. I have a low tolerance for frustration.
    a. Strongly agree   c. Moderately disagree
    b. Moderately agree   d. Strongly disagree

18. I get bored easily with routine tasks and thrive on challenges.
    a. Strongly agree   c. Moderately disagree
    b. Moderately agree   d. Strongly disagree

19. It is important for me to be the best in things I undertake to do.
    a. Strongly agree   c. Moderately disagree
    b. Moderately agree   d. Strongly disagree

20. I would choose to work with a difficult but highly competent person rather than a congenial but less competent one.
    a. Strongly agree   c. Moderately disagree
    b. Moderately agree   d. Strongly disagree

21. My age is:
    a. 20 to 28
    b. 29 to 37
    c. 38 to 46
    d. 47 or above

22. I have had _____ of experience in the industry in which I plan to start a business.
    a. 0 years
    b. 1/2 to 1 year
    c. 1 to 2 years
    d. More than 2 years

23. I have had the following business experience:
    a. A management position in a successful firm
    b. A management position in any firm
    c. No management experience

24. I have missed _____ days of work due to illness over the past three years.
    a. 0 to 5
    b. 6 to 10
    c. 11 to 15
    d. 16 or above

25. I generally need at least _____ hours of sleep to function effectively.
    a. 8
    b. 7
    c. 6
    d. 5 or less

How to Score

1. (a=4, b=3, c=2, d=1)
2. (a=4, b=3, c=2, d=1)
3. (a=4, b=3, c=2, d=1)
4. (a=4, b=3, c=2, d=1)
5. (a=4, b=3, c=2, d=1)
6. (a=4, b=3, c=2, d=1)
7. (a=4, b=3, c=2, d=1)
8. (a=1, b=2, c=3, d=4)
9. (a=4, b=3, c=2, d=1)
10. (a=4, b=3, c=2, d=1)
11. (a=4, b=3, c=2, d=1)
12. (a=1, b=2, c=3, d=4)
13. (a=4, b=3, c=2, d=1)
14. (a=4, b=3, c=2, d=1)
15. (a=4, b=3, c=2, d=1)
16. (a=4, b=3, c=2, d=1)
17. (a=1, b=2, c=3, d=4)
18. (a=4, b=3, c=2, d=1)
19. (a=4, b=3, c=2, d=1)
20. (a=4, b=3, c=2, d=1)
21. (a=2, b=4, c=3, d=1)
22. (a=1, b=2, c=3, d=4)
23. (a=4, b=3, c=1)
24. (a=4, b=3, c=2, d=1)
25. (a=1, b=2, c=3, d=4)

TRY IT HIS WAY

If you get a lemon, make lemonade. If you get dirt, make a shirt. That's what Robert Hedin did. After his first shirt company was destroyed by Hurricane Iniki in 1992, he started over only to find himself battling Mother Nature again. This time, it was Hawaii's red dirt which kept mucking up the shirts in the warehouse. Instead of throwing them out and eating the loss, he ended up using the dirt to dye the shirts, thus creating Red Dirt Shirts, and eventually an entire Red Dirt sportswear line. What's the lesson here? Create your own opportunities out of the challenges life throws your way.

What Your Score Means

94-100: What are you waiting for? You possess most, if not all, of the key personality and behavioral traits of the entrepreneur. You have the best chance to succeed.

85-93: A good bet. You possess most of the characteristics of an entrepreneur. If your score on the last five questions was 16 or above, it's possible that your behavioral attitudes will compensate for any personality traits you are lacking.

75-84: Risky business. You possess some entrepreneurial traits but probably not to the degree necessary to buck the daunting odds.

If your score on the last five questions was 15 or below, the risk is even greater. Remember: Entrepreneurs are not attracted to risk; they are attracted to challenges and opportunities. Keep working for someone else—you may be premature in your desire to be an entrepreneur.

Below 75: Stay right where you are. You possess an insufficient number and degree of the personality and behavioral patterns common to thriving entrepreneurs.

Keep the Faith

So what if you did poorly on the test? Well, if it doesn't dissuade you, then you still have the most important element you'll need—the drive to do it. Starting a small business is an exhilarating experience, and having the will to make it succeed is the single most important thing you'll need.

ASSESSING *your* experience *and* SKILLS

You don't have to be a business wizard to be an entrepreneur. Many successful businesses begin with someone who has an array of **talents,** experience, and **skills,** and knows where to go for help to fill in the gaps.

In fact, you've probably got more of all that than you realize. Your experience is the cumulative effect of what you've learned about specific businesses or areas of interest over time. Your skills are the particular talents and expertise that you've developed on your own time, or have been using to make money for someone else.

Building on Your Experience

A successful entrepreneur has solid knowledge of the business she is starting. After all, that's what your customers are paying for—your knowledge.

MOONLIGHTING

One way to get a taste of what starting and running a business is all about is to moonlight while you're still working your full-time gig. You can ease into the whole process slowly while you still have the security and benefits of your job.

If you've got a job that offers benefits and a pension plan, giving it all up to face the uncertainties of self-employment may be too risky. That's why so many entrepreneurs get their start in college by launching a little business on the side—they've got room and board paid for, and it's far less risky to give it a go part-time.

Here's a suggestion: Start a mini business, maybe a business that's very different from the one you'd ideally start. But the discipline and practice you get from running a little mail order company or doing taxes for friends on weekends may give you the insight you need to take the leap.

Don't be fooled by those ads that tell you that you can build a billion-dollar business without knowing anything about it. You need to have a broad understanding of who is going to buy your product or service and all the steps it takes to do the job professionally. A plumber needs to know where to get the right pipes and fittings, how to link them all together with nary a leak, how much to spend on supplies, how much the customer is willing to pay, what the local building codes are, and hundreds of other major and minor details about the business of plumbing. She also needs to know the details of running a small business, such as how to promote herself, keep the books, track inventory, and hire help.

But don't be intimidated by all that you may not know—once you realize what you don't have, you can buy it, rent it, hire it, or learn it. And learning as much as you can is a great way to start. For example, if you want to open a restaurant, bus tables and work in a restaurant's business office. You'd be surprised how much information you can absorb just by being present, and you have an excellent opportunity to see what techniques work and what can be improved. You can also ask questions and observe people. Not only will you get the experience, you'll also get a chance to decide if this business is something you really like. Even if you volunteer your services, the experience you gain will be invaluable.

Another way to get experience is to take courses and training sessions. You don't have to have an MBA to start your own business. Community col-

lege courses and continuing education programs offer concrete information, practical experience, and an opportunity to ask questions from someone in the know. Take one class at a time to fill in the gaps in your knowledge, or earn a program certificate to add to your list of credentials.

Transferring Your Experience

You don't necessarily have to limit yourself to the industry you're in now in order to capitalize on your experience. Many entrepreneurs are able to transfer what they've learned about business in general to their particular venture. For example, if you've spent ten years working in a flower shop, you probably understand what it takes to run a low-overhead retail establishment. These are things any local retailer can use.

Capitalizing on Your Skills

Make an honest assessment of your skills so you can find the best place for yourself in your new venture. Take a day to think about what you do well.

A start-up is as good as its people, and you're the key employee. What are your strengths? Here's a checklist:

- Creative

- Industrious

- Fast

- Good planner

DON'T GIVE UP

Wired magazine is a legendary overnight success story. Its success has led to the development of a major Web site, a line of books, a whole new look for advertising, and a major investment from Condé Nast.

But was it really an overnight success? No. The two founders of *Wired* spent years pitching the magazine. They met with hundreds of potential backers and were rejected hundreds of times. They talked to lawyers, magazines, bankers, investors—anyone who would take a meeting. It was only a chance meeting with a new-media guru from MIT that led to their eventual launch—years after they had conceived of the idea.

Turning a Hobby into a Business

If you're thinking it would be fun to transform something you play at into a business, be careful.

There are ways to do this, but you need to keep in mind that just because you love doing something doesn't necessarily mean it will make a successful business. In almost every case, you'll discover that you spend almost no time doing your hobby and lots of time selling it.

Entrepreneurs who have managed to make a go of it agree that the key to making it work is to separate the pleasure from the business. Knowing how to run around a tennis court, for example, will not necessarily give you the skills you need to run a tennis club.

Here are tips that might help:
• Get some real hands-on experience working in the field before you commit yourself. Be a part-time employee at an entry-level position, if necessary, to get an idea of the inner workings of the business. You'll get a very different picture working on the other side of the fence.

• Get lots of advice from experts who have had experience in the particular industry that interests you. Spending time with people who have worked in the field will really help fill in any of your knowledge gaps.

• If you're planning to have a partner, be sure it's someone who knows the ropes. If you choose another hobbyist as a partner, it could end up being a case of the blind leading the blind.

• Consult owners of other businesses in the field located in other cities. They won't be direct competitors and they may be able to provide you with valuable advice.

- Motivator

- Visionary

- Salesperson

- Talented (cook, sculptor, artist, writer, and so on)

- Networker

These are specific, practical skills that you can use as the foundation for your new business—because it is natural to open a business that emphasizes what you do best.

Here are some general business skills that you should have, and who will need to help you if you are not prepared to develop the skills yourself.

If You're Not	Find
Organized	A secretary or administrative assistant
Good with numbers	Someone to handle your finances
A good writer or artist	Help with sales proposals, advertising, promotion, publicity, marketing
Comfortable in social situations	Someone to deal with your clients and suppliers
Knowledgeable about legal requirements	Good legal advice

Supplementing Your Skills and Experience

When you think about starting a business, it conjures images of striking out on your own. The reality is you can't possibly do it all by yourself. Even if you run a one-person shop, it is absolutely vital that you seek out people who can supplement your skills and experiences. You'll need them to help you handle the initial details of setting up a business and the day-to-day details of running it. In fact, alliances with experienced, respected, or networked people can make your business grow faster, more profitably, and more reliably than it ever could on its own.

To begin, you'll need competent professionals, like an accountant to lead you through the number maze and a lawyer to guide you through the legal jungle. You don't have to

hire them full-time, although you may eventually want to. But you'll certainly want to consult with them before beginning, and rely on their services as you progress. Ideally these people should be more than just business advisers. They should be people you can trust. Because in addition to the factual information you have to get from them, you need reliable friends to have lunch with, bounce ideas off of, and confide in.

Although you can always open the phone book to find professionals who can help you, the best way is to build relationships with as many business people as you can. Go to trade association meetings. Visit chambers of commerce. Attend workshops and seminars. And everywhere you go, cultivate those friends so you can build a support system of knowledgeable people. It pays to learn from their experiences so you won't duplicate their mistakes, and you'll find many good people with lots of important skills.

Sooner or later, you'll want to consult with the Small Business Administration (SBA). It's a tremendous resource that can help answer almost any business question you can think of. This huge federal agency with about 80 field and district offices spread all over the country was created by Congress to help entrepreneurs find financing, training, general information, and advocacy.

The SBA also offers the Service Corps of Retired Executives (SCORE), a well-trained army of retired executives who volunteer their time and considerable expertise to provide budding and full-grown entrepreneurs with one-on-one confidential counseling, workshops, and training programs on how to obtain financing, organize channels of distribution, conduct market research, and other issues you'll need to know all about in order to get your business off the ground. (For information on locating the SCORE office nearest you, contact SCORE at (202) 205-6762.)

SCORE proved to be instrumental for Joseph, who had worked for 12 years as the point man for a medical supply business before starting out on a similar venture of his own. Joseph knew everything about buying and supplying the best equipment, had a knack for developing great relationships with customers, and even handled the purchasing and payroll responsibilities. But the prospect of risking his personal savings and family's future on a desire to run a similar business on his own terms sometimes seemed a little overwhelming. Through the SBA he was able to find a capable community lawyer with experience in setting up small businesses, an exceptionally

The Importance of Management Skills

Management skills include organizational abilities, a deftness for planning, and a penchant for decision making.

Every day you will be besieged with an incredible number of choices that will impact the outcome of business—from hiring employees to selecting a location or building for your shop, to selecting suppliers you can count on consistently.

There are no rules. There's no guaranteed right way of doing anything in business. That's why experience is so vital, and so are advisers. One thing that you can't delegate, though, is the ability to manage people—both employees and outsiders.

This isn't just about managing your employees and making sure they do things like get to work on time. People management is about dealing with your suppliers, your business partners, and your customers, too.

You've also got to be able to manage your customers' expectations. It isn't good business practice to promise a product or service that you can't deliver. Customers, like suppliers, have great long-term memory for those times when they've been disappointed. You want to be sure you operate with honesty and integrity—it's free and it's effective. And if you don't level with people, your business won't survive for very long.

There are hundreds of books, seminars, and other resources to help you understand the management of people. Some of them are listed in the resources section of this book. Invest in learning what you'll need to know—it will be vital to the growth of your business.

MAKE SURE YOU'LL ENJOY IT

With all the energy you're going to have to devote to a business, it's important to be sure that whatever you decide to do, it's something you enjoy. But make sure that before you open the doors, you consider some of the other factors involved in running a business.

Although you may love gardening, the irregular hours and seasonal demands of running a nursery may not offer you the same satisfaction as publishing a seed and garden supply catalog. If you love animals, you may want to consider opening a pet supply store. But keep in mind that you'll be spending all of your time inside and that there might be long stretches of time when you'll be in the store with no customers to serve. If you love the outdoors, maybe you should open a kennel instead of a retail store.

It's about your life and how you live it. Take some time to think about what you really like to do and what you want your day to be like.

competitive rate on a bank loan, and, perhaps most importantly, the ear of an entrepreneur who had started a similar business in another state 22 years earlier. Although Joseph started out knowing quite a bit about his business, the experienced entrepreneur was able to give Joseph valuable tips about purchasing equipment, timing his marketing, and finding the light at the end of the tunnel during rough times.

Moving on to the Plan

Once you've given serious thought to your skills and experiences, and how you can take advantage of the advice and strengths other people can bring to your business, it is time to sit down and put together a concrete plan, using the steps in chapter three.

CHARTING *your* business COURSE

*It's not enough to start a business and hope for the best. You need to map out a specific **plan**. By making a blueprint for the foreseeable future, you can get this whole thing in perspective and make it seem a little **less daunting.***

This is the biggest and most challenging job you've ever had. With all you have to manage, it's easy to get submerged in the details. But if you work out a strategy, you'll be able to break it down into manageable parts. So here's your five-step plan for starting your own business. It's not foolproof, because nothing is. But it's all the essentials in a nutshell. You get a preview here and details in the following chapters.

Step One: Make a Plan

You need a business plan. A business plan is a vital part of your start-up process. It consists of an overview of your company, an analysis of your market, discussions of the research and development of your product, marketing and sales strategies, a list of

personnel, and an outline of financial data. Your business plan is important for three reasons: It's tremendously valuable in clarifying for you what you're selling, what you need to spend to open your doors to the public, how much of that money you already have (and how much you're going to have to get from outside sources), and what structure your business is going to take (sole proprietorship, partnership, or corporation). It also plays a vital role in getting that outside financing, if you need it, because anyone who invests in your business or loans you money is going to want to see a business plan. And finally, the business plan will serve as your own reference tool. Because it contains so many details about your company, it will be enormously helpful in showing you just what you need to pull this whole thing together.

BUSINESS INFORMATION CENTERS (BICS)

Business Information Centers, located throughout the country, provide all kinds of free help to new and existing small businesses. You can get counseling and training in marketing and sales, pricing, exports, and creating a business plan, as well as access to business software, CD-ROMS, videotapes, and print reference materials. For a list of BICs around the country, see the resources section in the back of this book. New ones open every month, so for more information, call (202) 205-6665.

Step Two: Where's Your Cash?

You need a cash flow analysis. Like a business plan, it focuses on a critical issue you'll need to consider.

Step Three: Position Your Business and Your Product

What exactly does the product or service you create do to stand out? Why does it deserve to exist? Is it cheaper, faster, easier, more expensive, better, longer-lasting, sexier, endorsed, guaranteed, or what? Positioning is the art of describing the benefits you offer in a simple, cogent way that blocks your competition from your slot. For example, Tom's of Maine successfully postitioned its toothpaste as the only all-natural product on the market. This is so important there's more on it later.

Tap into the Resources of the SBA

The Small Business Administration (SBA) is an independent agency of the U.S. government that aids, counsels, assists, and protects the interests of small businesses. It works with banks and other lending institutions to provide loans and venture capital financing to small businesses unable to get financing through other sources. In addition to the 7(a) Loan Guarantee Program, the SBA's primary lending program, it offers a variety of other financing alternatives designed to meet the specific needs of entrepreneurs, including:

• Small Business Investment Companies (SBICs), privately owned and managed investment firms, licensed and regulated by the SBA, that provide start-up and venture capital

• LowDoc, a streamlined loan review process for loans under $100,000

• Microloans, for small loans from $100 to $25,000

• Certified Development Company Program (504 Loan), long-term financing for purchasing land, buildings, machinery, equipment

The SBA also administers Small Business Development Centers, which provide management assistance to new and existing business owners in the form of counseling, training, and technical assistance. (See page 25 for details.)

For more information, visit the Small Business Administration Web site (http://www.sba.gov) or call (800) 827-5722 for the regional office nearest you.

LOW-COST SBA BUSINESS COURSES AND WORKSHOPS

Here's a sample of some SBA programs (and the cost) offered over a six-month period in the New York metropolitan area: Financing for Small Business (Free), Marketing Your Products/Services ($30), Business Planning Workshop (Free), Starting and Managing Your Business ($20), Marketing Principles for Small Business (Free), International Trade ($10), Business Plans and Loan Packaging (Free).

This is just a sample of what's offered. Visit this SBA Web site for information about similar programs in your area: http://www.sba.gov

Do these three things before you spend a dollar! Chapter six will show you how to get these essential documents written.

Step Four: Identify Your Goals

Defining clear objectives for your business provides you with an operating framework. You can use it as a point of reference to help keep you on target and give you a sense of your progress along the way. Aim high, but be realistic. For some businesses, it's an accomplishment to break even in the first year. And when you're looking at sales figures, it's a good idea to use your past performance working for other people as a guide. It may be exhilarating to project first-year sales at $1 million, but if you've never seen those figures before, it's probably not going to happen.

A good way to structure your objectives is to divide them into short-term (a few months from now), mid-range (your first year), and long-term (five to ten years down the road) goals. The general categories suggested here should be used as a guide. You may have other issues you need to address. You can adapt this to suit your business.

Short-Term Goals: The First Few Months

Your goals for the first few months are literally the things you need to get you up and running. They're important, because they help lay the groundwork for the next few years. Take a look:

Small Business Development Centers

The Small Business Development Center (SBDC) Program is a network of information and guidance services administered by the U.S. Small Business Administration (SBA). There are close to 1,000 locations across the country—as well as the District of Columbia, Guam, Puerto Rico, and the U.S. Virgin Islands—that provide small businesses with free management and technical support.

Potential and existing small businesses can receive help with financing, marketing, production, engineering, technical problems, feasibility studies, international trade, and personnel management.

Because SBDCs are funded partially by the SBA and partially by matching fund sponsors from the public and private sectors, SBDCs very often provide the same services at no charge that private business consulting firms offer for thousands of dollars. Sponsors include state legislatures, private foundations and grants, chambers of commerce, universities, vocational and technical schools, and community colleges.

For information about the SBDC location nearest you, contact the Small Business Answer Desk at (800) 8-ASK-SBA (827-5722) or visit the SBA online at http://www.sba.gov

- *Capital*. A major cause of business failure is an insufficiency of start-up capital. The SBA advises that after you have paid for equipment and real estate, you should have enough to cover the first year's operating expenses.

  Calculate how much of that you already have and how much you need to borrow. Identify your potential sources (family and friends, bank loans, venture capitalists) and decide which is the best place to obtain financing and how soon you need it to begin your operations.

- *Office space*. If you're not planning a home-based business, how soon can you find office space and move in? If you have to do extensive renovations, factor in the time it will take to get the space ready.

- *Equipment*. What type of equipment will you need? This includes things like telephones, faxes, copiers, and computers as well as production machinery. Will you be leasing or purchasing it? Do you have your sources of supply? How soon can you expect to have the equipment operational?

- *Staffing*. How many people will you need to make this enterprise work? Do you have sufficient contacts to hire them or will you be using the services of an employment agency? Can your staffing requirements be fulfilled by using contractors or freelancers or do you need full- or part-time employees?

- *Opening your doors*. How quickly after you obtain financing, set up your equipment, and arrange for staff will you be able to actually begin your operations? You should aim for this to happen as soon as possible because you need to be producing income to offset your expenses.

- *Sales*. This doesn't necessarily have to be a dollar figure, especially for the first few months. You can think in terms of how many contacts you expect to make, how many proposals you plan to send out, and how many sales calls you complete.

- *Shipping*. Will you be mailing your product or do you need to arrange for trucking? If you need a truck, will you be buying or leasing it and how soon will it be available?

- *Advertising/promotion/publicity.* How soon can you get a logo set up and signs made? Do you need to use outside advertising and public relations agencies or can you produce the necessary pieces in-house?

Mid-Range Goals: The First Year

Once you've got your seed money, an office, the equipment you need, and your staff, you're really ready to cook. Now you have to think about what you want to accomplish in the next 12 months.

- *What are your first-year sales projections?* You should expect to realize actual sales figures within the first year, reaping the benefits of all those contacts, proposals, and advertising. This figure is not carved in stone, and it's subject to change with new developments, but it helps to have a concrete objective so you can keep on track from month to month.

- *When do you expect to show a profit?* This may happen within the first year, but it's possible that a more realistic scenario would be to see profits somewhere later down the road. Keep in mind when you're drawing a profit picture that a business venture is an overall long-term proposition.

CATALOG OF FEDERAL DOMESTIC ASSISTANCE

This catalog lists and describes all of the programs, projects, services, and activities provided by federal government agencies to help the public, including those intended to assist small business owners. You can search the listings on the World Wide Web for free at http://www.gas.gov/fdac/ or purchase the searchable text in hard copy, tape, floppy diskettes, or CD-ROM formats from:

Federal Domestic Assistance Catalog Staff (MVS)
General Services Administration
300 Seventh St. SW
Suite 101
Washington, DC 20407
(202) 708-5126.

Case Study: Gary D'Alessandro Hair and Nail Care Center

Sure, you say. This stuff looks good on paper. But if I do all this, can it really work? Will I really be able to start my own business by following these steps? It can and you will. And here's a true story to prove it.

Nine years ago, Gary D'Alessandro was working as a hairstylist in someone else's shop. The owner offered to make him a partner, but the deal fell through. By that time, he had been bitten by the entrepreneur bug and decided he couldn't be happy unless he went out on his own. He had tried it once, and the business had failed. But this time, he was determined to do it right.

Gary is another successful business owner who says he was lucky. Be that as it may, he took advantage of the powerful networking opportunities he already had at his fingertips while he was working for someone else. One of his clients was a market researcher—she did a study for him that identified a wealthy, growing community that had a need for an upscale hair salon. There were two other hairdressers in the town, but neither was supplying the kind of sophisticated service and styling Gary could offer.

Based on that information, he chose to position himself as the most upscale hairdresser in town. He brainstormed with another client—a prominent interior designer and entrepreneur herself—over a six-month period. She and her husband helped him map out an informal business plan. A third client was an attorney, who helped him select a business structure (S corporation) and draw up the papers.

Gary opened his doors over nine years ago, yet he still takes time to educate himself through seminars sponsored by his suppliers. He also reads trade publications and takes business courses at the local community college. And although it took three years for Gary to see a profit—a period of time during which he made far less money than when he was working for someone else—he never gave up. And now his business is thriving.

Gary claims that his secret to success was realizing early on that the people in his community want personalized service. They don't mind paying a little more, and because they have the financial resources to go anywhere, they will reject anything that doesn't scream quality. So Gary trains his employees to treat his customers with the degree of attention they expect. And he delivers what they want.

Gary's advice to fellow small business adventurers: "Don't ever be afraid to ask anybody for anything. One of my biggest fears was asking people for help. Once I got over that, the doors just flew open."

- *Repayment timetable.* The sooner you can pay off those initial loans, the more working capital you'll have available.

- *Product line.* Do you plan to expand enough in the first year to consider adding new products? This should be somewhat flexible, as many business owners find they add products as they discover demand for them.

- *Personnel.* Do you anticipate an increase in staff or hiring contractors or freelancers? Try to be as specific as possible here when you calculate your requirements so you can allocate enough expenses.

- *Advertising/promotion/publicity.* This is the time to start thinking about a more aggressive marketing campaign. Keep in mind that there are ways to be cost-efficient about promoting your products. Decide whom you want to reach and the most effective means to achieve visibility.

Long-Range Goals: Five to Ten Years

Where do you see your business five or even ten years from now? Are you thinking in terms of challenging the industry giant, or will you be happy with a small, more intimate operation?

- *Sales projections.* Be sure to factor in any growth potential in your market.

- *Personnel.* With an increase in sales, will you need to add people to your sales staff to keep up with an expanding production?

- *Office space.* Do you anticipate an expansion that will require more space? It might be to your advantage to take more space than you need initially and sublet part of it.

- *Expansion possibilities.* Think about different ways to increase your market share, either geographically, or by adding similar or related products, or adding services that support your products.

The Strange Case of Dr. X

This is a story about a girl who was raised to be a doctor. From the time she was old enough to understand, she thought she was going to practice medicine. She was bright. She got good grades. She did especially well in science. Her parents paid for college, put her through medical school, and watched proudly as she progressed through the academic system, passing all the exams and placing high in her class.

But she had two problems. First, she had no people skills—she was very intuitive, she had a sharp, clinical mind, and the makings of a great diagnostician, but she could not communicate effectively with patients. The second, more serious obstacle to her success as a doctor was that she discovered halfway through medical school that she hated touching people's bodies.

For fear of disappointing her parents, she hung on until almost the very end. She was a resident, one month away from graduation, when she announced to family and friends that she could not be a doctor. It took courage to change direction after she had invested so much. But she was lucky that she had the instinct to recognize she was not suited to the profession everyone expected to her to follow. She decided to turn her skills and talents to medical research, a field that makes the best use of her personality and temperament.

The point is it's absolutely vital to pick a business that will allow you to do the things you enjoy—and to avoid like the plague a business that will require you to do things you're uncomfortable with.

By defining your expectations, you'll get a clear picture of what you have to do to meet them. This road you're on is filled with potholes and detours. Make a timetable (subject to revision, of course, as circumstances dictate). Your schedule of events will remind you of your priorities and help you deal with the problems you come across along the way.

Step Five: Get Financing

You will probably have to use some of your own money to get your business off the ground. But you will no doubt need more. There are all kinds of sources, from private investors and venture capitalists to bank loans, commercial finance companies, local development companies, and the Small Business Administration. Chapter seven will explore these options in detail.

Step Six: Get Ready, Get Set, Get Started!

Once you've chosen your product, positioned it, written a business plan, and obtained the necessary financing, you can finally get down to the nitty gritty details of operating your business. You'll need to choose a city or community, and if you're not home-based, a specific site within that community. Chapter six will show you how to do all that, as well as find suppliers, price your product, get insurance, deal with taxes, and hire your employees.

POSITIONING *your* business *and your* PRODUCT

CHAPTER FOUR

Last year, in the grocery store alone, there were more than 17,000 new products introduced. With that much noise, the chances of being noticed are small. And the chance of being remembered is almost zero.

As you launch your business, you'll need to remind yourself that no one cares as much about what you do as you do! Don't expect your prospects to spend the time to learn everything there is to know about you. It won't happen. They might give you a second, they might give you a minute—but then your business, your benefits, the features of what you do have to stick in their mind.

Two brilliant marketers, Jack Trout and Al Reis, wrote a breakthrough book called *Positioning*. Their thesis is that every individual takes a second to consider a new idea, a new business, a new person. Then the person either discards the information or stores it in a position in his brain. And no two ideas can occupy the same position.

POSITIONING A PET STORE

When Marianne opened a small pet shop, she knew she had to distinguish it somehow from the two big discount pet shops in the area which were able to sell their products for less and had more of a variety. So Marianne took a totally different approach. She noticed that her customers tended to hang out and talk to her and each other about their pets. She decided to offer services that the big stores didn't—like pet sitting and pet care advice. She put up a bulletin board on which people could place messages about vets, kennels, and dog-friendly parks in the area and did a great job of positioning her store as a friendly, intimate place where people could come and schmooze.

Seven Up is the very best example of a company that did this properly. It had no chance in the world of usurping Coke or Pepsi's positions in people's minds. So it decided to use the strength of these brands against them. By positioning itself as the UnCola, the stronger Coke got, the stronger Seven Up got. It was Coke, but without the color, without the caffeine, without the heaviness.

Every successful business occupies a great position with its happy clients. You have to stand for something (dependable overnight delivery, the friendliest neighborhood vet, the inexpensive graphic designer) if you want someone to give you a position.

Another word for this is "niche." A hole. A crevice. A place where you can fit in. You can either choose your company's niche or people will choose it for you (or worse, ignore you!). We paint houses is not a niche. It's a description of what you'd like to do. We paint Victorian houses, on the other hand, is very much a niche. It's a slot you can own, something you can specialize in.

People without Victorian houses don't need you, don't want you, and don't care. That's fine. Because by focusing your energy on the people who do, you can quickly become the best choice.

How Do You Pick a Niche?

Your position should be defensible. Don't be so broad that you'll invite competition you can't compete with. At the same time, don't be so narrow that even with 100 percent of the market, you still can't make a living.

For example, if you're a copyeditor, you could specialize in medical journals, best selling novels or neighborhood flyers. By picking an audience and marketing to it, you're much more likely to reach the critical mass you need to become profitable. On the other hand, specializing in maritime novels written in Norwegian will probably win you some loyal customers, but it's unlikely you'll be able to support the family.

The best niches are the ones that are growing. That way, you can let the rising tide carry you along, instead of having to constantly reinvent yourself to get more business. Finding a growing niche can be challenging, but if you can spot the trends, it'll be worth the effort.

How Do You Spot the Trends?

The best way to spot trends is to get informed. Read the business sections of your local newspapers, as well as *The Wall Street Journal* and *Barron's.* Check the classified ads for products and types of businesses that appeal to you. By perusing these pages, you'd be surprised at how many ideas you can get. A recent edition of the business section of *The New York Times,* for example, had articles about:

- A hospital rating service

- The funeral business (euphemistically referred to as the "death care" industry)

TRY IT HIS WAY

David Eisenhaure, chairman of SatCon Technology, a Cambridge, Massachusetts based electromechanical company, talks about his "elevator" theory. Although his firm makes highly specialized technology products, Eisenhaure says he can describe SatCon's mission to anyone he's standing next to in an elevator before the doors open on the person's floor. He explains that SatCon manufactures devices that make machines more intelligent. This technique of reducing the complex to the simple has helped finance types, employees, and public relations people understand his mission. Take the challenge. Can you tell your company story to a complete stranger in less than a minute? It's an exercise to help keep your positioning statement focused and to the point. Try it on your next elevator ride.

THE RULE OF POSITIONING

If you provide a product or service that's just like an existing product or service, you will probably not succeed. You need to be faster, more varied, slower, cheaper, easier to work with, prettier, more highly recommended, or longer lasting. Entrepreneurs rarely have enough capital to beat an entrenched competitor at her own game.

- Electric cars

- Private prisons

Of course, none of these may be the business for you, but the point is that every issue features different industries and eventually you'll see certain issues coming up again and again. If you're reading and hearing a lot about certain businesses and industries, it means they're probably going places.

Once you've isolated a trend, go to the experts— the trade magazines and newspapers that cover that industry. Did you know that you could subscribe to *Pizza Today* or *Computer Gaming World*? Read dozens of back issues and you'll discover who's advertising, who's hiring, who's shrinking, and where the niches might be.

It can't hurt to join some trade organizations as well. Gale Research publishes the *Encyclopedia of Associations*. The national edition lists 23,000 trade, professional, civic, and cultural associations, and is available in the reference section of most public libraries or by contacting Gale Research at (800) 877-4253.

And get wired. The Internet is full of resources for budding business owners. From online magazines to access to the Small Business Administration Web site (http://www.sba.gov) and other government agencies, you can get an amazing amount of insight into industry and market trends.

Researching the Market

Once you've narrowed down the field to a particular business or industry, you need to get specific information about your customers and their buying patterns as well as details about your competition's strategies, strengths, and weaknesses. This doesn't necessarily have to be in a formal report format, although there are market research

companies that will conduct surveys (for a fee). They can provide information on the size of the market, growth predictions, an analysis of the competition, and distribution channels. For a list of market researchers in your industry or area as well as access to publications and books about market research, contact:

Marketing Research Association
2189 Silas Deane Highway, Suite 5
P.O. Box 230
Rocky Hill, CT 06067
(860) 257-4008

There are also places to find valuable information about your market inexpensively. The same sources that provide general market insights have detailed analyses as well. By reading business magazines like *Business Week, Inc., Crain's Small Business,* and *Entrepreneur,* you gain access to the results of various surveys in addition to general overviews of markets. Chambers of commerce can provide information on your competition in the form of statistics on the size of their operations, including details about the number of employees, the size of their facility, and even consumer complaints.

TRY IT HIS WAY

When his customers complained, Ernie Cruwell responded. That's how Ernie's Shopping Cart Specialties began. The way his shopping cart corrals were originally designed, they were difficult to ship and assemble. So he solved the problem by creating a unique product—a collapsible shopping cart corral that ships inexpensively and sets up by unfolding. His business is so successful, he managed to sell $1 million worth of corrals in 1996 based solely on customer referrals.

Positioning: Cutting through the Clutter

Once you know all about your market, you take that information and translate it into a position for your business. Positioning is about taking control of your business right from the start. The trick is to figure out what's different and special about what you have to offer so that you're the one they think of when they're ready to buy.

TRY IT HER WAY

Gerri Mack wanted her
three little girls to wear out-
fits that looked like they
belonged on kids. But all
she saw when she shopped
were scaled-down adult
clothes, and she was getting
tired of trying to find a
wardrobe she deemed
appropriate. So she decided
to start a line of children's
clothing that really works for
kids. Other people must
agree with her, because
they're buying her Mack &
Moore designs at over 700
stores (including
Bloomingdale's, Neiman
Marcus, and Nordstrom)
and through some mail
order catalogs as well. She
fills a marketing need to the
tune of $2 million a year.

Step One

Identify one of your potential customer's problems and figure out a way to fix it. Listen carefully
to the complaints of your potential clients about
the products they use. In fact, emphasize this solution as a benefit that customers can receive by
doing business with you. The management of
D'Agostino, a New York City supermarket,
noticed that in family neighborhoods, parents
were cutting their shopping trips short when their
young children got bored and cranky. By providing an infant/toddler room for them to drop off
their tots to be entertained by a babysitter, the parents could shop leisurely—loading up more gro-
ceries and spending more money. D'Agostino
positioned itself as the kid-friendly supermarket.

Step Two

Focus on a small segment of the market. You can't
be all things to all people. It's hard enough to be
really good at one thing. So concentrate on what
you're good at and target the part of the market
that needs that product or service. In the crowded
field of interior designers, Amanda has established
herself as an expert working with clients who have relatively small budgets. She
charges them a flat fee instead of getting a percentage of the furniture sales, rearranges
some of the pieces that these people already own, and helps them find bargains in
inexpensive furniture stores like Workbench and Ikea. She's been successful at minimizing her clients' expenses, she gives their digs brand-new looks, and in the process,
she has created a name for herself as a user-friendly interior designer for people on a
budget.

Step Three

Find the industry giant's flaw. No product or service is perfect and consumers can always find something to beef about—even the big guys are not immune. Maybe you're thinking of opening an inn in a resort town. Look carefully at the biggest hotel in the area. In this case its size alone makes it vulnerable to attack. It can't possibly be intimate, personal, cozy—all the things that you are. Play against this. You're the place people want to go when they want to feel really taken care of. They'll get lots of attention, you check every detail, and you make them feel like they have a home away from home. That's your position.

Be Consistent

Once you've positioned your product, you need to promote it and advertise consistently. Your position becomes your signature. If you've opened Fresco, a kid-friendly, family restaurant that serves big portions and appeals to all generations, you want people to think of your restaurant every time they go out with the kids. Don't try to appeal to singles as well. Stick to your formula. Know what you are and do it well.

TRY IT HIS WAY

Mike Lee is an entrepreneur who keeps his typesetting customers happy by providing personal service. He accepts delivery of jobs by e-mail, "snail mail," overnight delivery services, or he will provide pick-up and delivery service himself, if necessary. Every job is returned with a thank-you note, instructions on handling to prevent damage, and sometimes a coupon for a discount on the next job. When people need a friendly, convenient, and fast typesetter, they think of Mike first.

The other thing about consistency is you need to convey your position in every advertisement and promotional item. Every printed piece that has your business name on it should also be used to telegraph this message. There are the obvious materials like brochures and direct mail pieces. But don't overlook things like invoices, business cards, letterhead, gift certificates, signs, checks, even labels and proposals. A couple of words that tell the world what you are and how you're different should be next to your company logo every time people see it.

TRY IT HIS WAY

Necessity is truly the mother of invention. That's what
rancher Jerry Gohl discovered one dark, freezing night
while tending his livestock.
What he needed, he
thought, was a portable,
remote-controlled spotlight
he could use from inside his
truck. When he tried to buy
one, though, he discovered
the thing didn't exist. So he
made one himself—and in
1996, he ended up selling
over $1 million worth of
these Golights to hunters,
boaters, and fishermen all
over the world.

Love Your Product

One final vital word of advice. Make sure you love
what you're doing and the position you've chosen.
If you're enthusiastic about what you're selling,
your belief in your product will be contagious.
When you present it—to employees, customers, in
promotion and advertising material—transmit a
sense of energy and excitement. You may have said
these things a thousand times, but you have to
make each delivery fresh and new. If you truly love
and believe in your business, you'll have little trouble keeping yourself energized, and your customers will be able to believe in it, too.

CHOOSING *your* business FORM

CHAPTER FIVE

About 75 percent of businesses are sole proprietor-ships. But partnerships, corporations, and even more **exotic** structures could be what you need. Your **choice** of a legal structure for your business has a lot to do with its management, financing, taxes, and level of risk.

Hundreds of years ago, a business was a person. If the business failed, the owner went to debtor's prison. Obviously, this wasn't doing a particularly good job of encouraging commerce.

Add to this the difficulty of finding investors, and you had a system that just wasn't working. So the government stepped in and developed a variety of legal fictions that keep lawyers busy and allow entrepreneurs a safety net and a simple way to share ownership.

INCORPORATION CONSULTANTS

The Company Corporation
1313 North Market St.
Wilmington, DE 19801
(302) 575-0440

Corporate Agents
1013 Center Road
Wilmington, DE 19805
(800) 877-4224

Delaware Business
Incorporators
3422 Old Capitol Trail
Suite 700
Wilmington, DE 19808
(800) 423-2993

Harvard Business Services
25 Greystone Manor
Lewes, DE 19958
(800) 345-2677

Part of the process of starting your business is deciding what legal form it will take. The form or structure of your business describes the way it's organized—who owns it, how profits and losses are divided, and how decisions are made. It also affects how you'll pay taxes and how easy it will be to grow the business. A few hours invested now could lead to millions of dollars in profits later.

Every company has a legal structure. The "Inc." behind a company's name tells you, for instance, that it takes the legal form of a corporation. Same with "Corp." There are lots of other forms. Here's the list: sole proprietorships, Subchapter S corporations, professional corporations (also called C corporations), limited liability corporations, partnerships, limited partnerships, joint ventures, and even nonprofit organizations.

Deciding on a legal structure is a matter of checking out several forms that are available to you, perhaps after consulting with experts. Once you have made up your mind, you'll need to do an amount of paperwork varying from none to quite a bit, depending on the form you've chosen. When you're done, your business will have taken on a legal life.

You can decide on a form now, before you craft your business plan, or you may be able to wait until later. It's probably not critical to your business—your customers, for instance, won't care. But it does make a difference to the IRS and to investors or other people who may join you in your venture. That makes it a significant decision—and doing it right the first time will save you time and money.

Here's a table of the different forms, along with pluses and minuses for each.

Form	Upside	Downside
Sole proprietorships	Easy	Liable for all debts, one owner
Professional corporations	For doctors and lawyers and the like	For doctors and lawyers and the like
Limited liability corporations	Liability protection, multiple owners	New, not recognized everywhere
Partnerships	Easy	Liable for all debts
Limited partnerships	Easy, investors not liable	Principal liable for all debts
Joint ventures	Easy	Not very useful
Nonprofit organizations	No taxes	No profits, lots of rules
Subchapter S corporations	Liability protection, multiple owners	Some limits
C Corporations	Can get very big, can go public	Double taxation

The first option to consider is the sole proprietorship, the fast, easy, simple alternative used by the majority of businesses in this country.

Sole Proprietorship

A sole proprietorship, also known as an individual proprietor or sole owner business, is a business that is owned by one person. The single owner gets to keep all the profits and is responsible for paying all the debts the business incurs.

To create a sole proprietorship, you don't have to do a thing other than open your doors, hang out your shingle, or otherwise start doing business. You don't need to fill out any complicated legal documents or pay any lawyers to get going. The ease and low cost of sole proprietorships makes them very attractive to start-ups.

Once you get going, everything is very straightforward. You own the company. You make the decisions. You get to keep the profits, which you report on your personal tax return, using a Schedule C, and which are taxed at your personal rate. If you decide not to continue the business, you pay everybody off, sell your assets, and lock the doors.

ONE-STOP SHOPPING FOR VIDEOS AND PUBLICATIONS

There really is so much information out there, it's hard to know where to start. *The Resource Directory for Small Business Management* is free and it's available from the SBA. Call the SBA Answer Desk at (800) 827-5722 for this listing of publications and videotapes you can purchase. It helps to have it all in one place.

A red tape caveat: Just because you're a sole proprietor doesn't make you exempt from *all* paperwork. If, like most entrepreneurs, you've given your business a name other than your own, you will need to register your business as an assumed name at your county courthouse. Depending on where you are, this may also be known as a doing-business-as or DBA form. Its purpose is to let everyone know that the Compleat Pet is the name under which Ben and Mary are doing business.

Other paperwork is also likely to pop up. If you're operating a restaurant, even as a sole proprietor, you'll probably need a health certificate. Many retail operations will need sales tax certificates. If you have employees, you'll need to get a federal tax ID number by filling out the IRS form SS-4.

Finally, while profits from sole proprietorships are generally not taxed aside from whatever personal taxes you pay, that's not always true. New York City, for instance, levies a special income tax called an unincorporated business tax on sole proprietorships.

The most paperless small business, in case you're wondering, is probably a one-person freelance personal services business. Only if you're a utility bill auditor, freelance writer, personal fitness trainer, or similar individual can you really hope to cut loose from red tape.

Despite the appeal of the sole proprietorship, there are good reasons why not every business is a sole proprietorship. It may not be for you if:

- *You're more than one person.* By definition, a sole proprietorship is for a business with a single owner. If you plan to share ownership with one or more others, a sole proprietorship isn't going to work.

- *You need to raise money from investors.* Investors usually want a share of ownership, which a sole proprietorship can't provide. So if you hope to raise capital by offering a piece of the action, a sole proprietorship isn't the form for your business.

One exception to the financing limitation: If you plan to raise capital by borrowing money, as opposed to trading part ownership for it, you may be able to do so as a sole proprietor. The caveat is that you'll be personally liable for the money you borrow for your business.

- *You will need to hire highly skilled key employees.* This is not a hard and fast rule, but often in-demand people prefer to work for companies where they can aspire to a share of the ownership. They won't find it in a job with a sole proprietor.

- *You are concerned about protecting yourself from liability.* This is one of the most important drawbacks to sole ownership. As a sole proprietor, you have unlimited liability for all debts. If your business runs up a bill it can't pay, your suppliers could, depending on your state laws, come after your savings, your car, and other personal assets.

HOW CAN STATE AND LOCAL ECONOMIC DEVELOPMENT AGENCIES HELP?

Economic development agencies are state and local government-operated departments that seek to encourage businesses to relocate or establish themselves in the area. To accomplish this, they often offer tax incentives, sponsor business incubation programs, relax zoning regulations, and provide other incentives. In addition, they are wonderful sources of information on markets and opportunities. Call your state and local governments to see if there's an economic development agency operating in your area.

Warning: Even though a sole proprietorship is easy and pretty streamlined, you need to be able to sleep at night. It's one thing if you're running a typing service or some other service business where the risks are low. But if you intend to have employees, offices, or big contracts, it's worth the hassle to protect yourself with a corporation.

Corporation

Corporations are favored by large companies. They are separate entities with a legal existence apart from their shareholders. In practice, that means a corporation is generally responsible for its own debts and other liabilities. You can sell a corporation, take it public, fold it, merge it, or just own it.

Corporations are straightforward to create. They are organized under the laws of each state and, generally, require only that you fill out some legal documents and pay a filing fee. You can obtain the basic forms to create a corporation at many stationery and office supply stores. If you need a little assistance, many manuals have been written describing the process step by step. And if you anticipate some complexity, such as adding more partners down the road, you can consult an attorney for advice. There are also dozens of filing services that will set you up for very little money.

Because of the filing fees and possible professional advice, a corporation is the most expensive form of business to create. While you may be able to do it yourself for under $100, creating a corporation with the help of an attorney could cost you from $1,000 to $3,000. Many entrepreneurs have found it both easier and less expensive to use an incorporation consultant. Give one of the ones listed on page 42 a call.

You definitely do get something for your money, however. Setting up as a corporation makes it easier to raise money. Corporations are allowed to sell shares. This can get messy, so don't do it without an expert attorney giving you advice. In the same way, you may be able to attract better employees when you can offer them a shot at owning a share of the business.

GO TO DELAWARE

Over 50 percent of Fortune 500 businesses have incorporated in the state of Delaware. Why? Two reasons, actually:

• It costs less. The fee to incorporate in Delaware can be as low as $74 and there is a host of tax and liability laws that can save businesses thousands of dollars each year.

• There are several laws on the books that limit the liability of corporations, making it a safer place to do business.

On the downside, control is more complicated. There are three layers of control. The shareholders (the owners) vote to decide important matters such as whether to sell the business. They also elect a board of directors that makes important policy decisions and elects the corporate officers. A corporate officer team usually consists of at least a president, secretary, and treasurer. These people sign contracts and otherwise run the business day-to-day. In most states, you can have just two people run the entire board, and just one person be the only shareholder, so you don't need a giant group to handle one.

In a standard corporation, the profits are taxed twice. This is a huge impediment to a small business. The corporation, as a separate entity, pays taxes on its profits. Then the owners also have to pay taxes on any dividends they earn from the profits. If you don't expect to reinvest most of the money you'll be making, it's probably a mistake. For every dollar in profit left over after salaries, you'll take home less than 50 cents.

OFFICE OF BUSINESS LIAISON

The U.S. Department of Commerce's Office of Business Liaison will supply you with a list of U.S. government programs designed to help businesses. For more information, contact:

U.S. Department of Commerce
Office of Business Liaison
14th St. and Constitution Ave. NW
Room 5898C
Washington, DC 20230
(202) 377-3176

Fortunately, there's a way around the double taxation. It's called an S corporation, and it's described below.

The paperwork that's part of running a corporation is more complicated than with other forms. In most states you have to file an annual report listing the corporation's name, address, and officers—and pay a fee. You'll also have to hold regular meetings and document them by recording the minutes. Think of a corporation as the corporate lawyer's full employment act.

Warning: There are some important limitations to the corporate veil that shield a corporation's owners from risking their personal assets. If the company goes broke, you could theoretically wash your hands and walk away. But banks and other lenders know

this. So they will often demand personal guarantees from a business owner before extending credit. Don't sign one unless you have absolutely no choice in the matter!

The owners may also be held liable if the debt results from a judgment in a lawsuit resulting from an action taken directly by one of them. This ability of sophisticated and determined lawyers to sometimes "pierce the corporate veil" is why you shouldn't place 100 percent of your faith in the liability reduction.

Subchapter S Corporation

Subchapter S corporations were set up for people who like everything about the corporation form but the double taxation. They're set up like corporations but taxed like partnerships. In fact, the only difference between an S corporation and a regular corporation (also called a C corporation) is the way it's taxed.

With an S corporation, all the profits flow directly to the owners. In essence, only you pay taxes, not the corporation as well.

There are some limitations to S corporations. You can only have up to 35 shareholders, none of whom may be another corporation. You can also issue only one class of stock. (Some C corporations issue nonvoting shares or other special classes.)

If you get very lucky and your business skyrockets, you can always switch from an S corporation to a C corporation.

Professional Corporation

Professional corporations are yet another kind of corporation. This form is usually available only for people who render professional services: accountants, architects, attorneys, dentists, doctors, and the like. It's probably not worth considering for the average small business owner.

Limited Liability Corporation

The limited liability corporation is a relatively new business structure and still only recognized by about two-thirds of the states. It's considered a corporation under state law and resembles an S corporation in many ways. Like an S corporation, it's taxed like a partnership, but limits liability like a C corporation.

One of the differences with an LLC, as it's also known, is that it's easier to add new owners than with an S. They can, for instance, have another corporation as shareholders.

LLCs can also distribute profits almost any way they like, rather than strictly by share of ownership. Likewise, they can generally agree to parcel out losses and deductions to the owners in whatever fashion will bring the owners the most benefit.

The limitations of LLCs are mainly due to their novelty. Some issues are still being sorted out, and if your state is one of those that doesn't recognize LLCs, you're out of luck. Ask your lawyer. If it works in your state, this is probably the way to go.

The following are some less common formats for your business.

Joint Venture

A joint venture is like a partnership with a limited lifespan. It's a good choice, for instance, if you plan to get together with someone else to buy a house, fix it up, and sell it. When the deal's done, so's the business.

There's no need to file any legal paperwork other than obtaining the usual licenses and tax certificates. But the same precautions about selecting a partner still apply. And just to avoid later misunderstandings, have a written agreement describing the purpose of the joint venture, who's going to

SBA ANSWER DESK

The SBA has a toll-free number that hooks you up to an automated system that directs you to sources of small business information. Call the SBA Answer Desk at (800) 827-5722.

TRY IT HIS WAY

A partnership is like a marriage; it's important for partners to complement each other. But with all the issues that are bound to come up, it's also important to choose a partner you are comfortable spending time with.

Paul Verrochi is an entrepreneur who has become an expert at choosing partners. He built American Medical Response (AMR), the nation's largest ambulance company, by acquiring over 150 smaller companies, and he treats each deal like a partnership.

One strategy he uses is to invite each company head to his home for a few days. It provides an opportunity for the prospective partners to learn a lot about each other as they share meals and socialize in an atmosphere outside the office. Verrochi says he has actually backed away from deals when he felt the chemistry wasn't right, and he's avoided making huge mistakes.

do what, how profits will be distributed, and when and how it will end.

Nonprofit Organization

Nonprofit organizations are generally churches, educational institutions, social welfare organizations, or perhaps industry associations. A nonprofit usually sets up as a corporation or a trust. (A trust is a fiduciary relationship between people in which one, called the trustee, holds title to a property for the benefit of the other, called the beneficiary.) Nonprofit corporations operate like other corporations, except that their income is tax-free.

Keep in mind: Nonprofit status is only for intentionally not-for-profit organizations. Just because your business fails to make a profit for a while doesn't mean you're not a for-profit entity. You'll have to get the IRS to qualify you as nonprofit.

Partnership

A partnership is an organization of two (or more) people who pool money, skills, energy, and other resources to form a business. They split the profits or, if things go badly, losses. And they are, individually and together, liable for the partnership's debts.

Like a sole proprietor, a partnership doesn't necessarily require filing any particular forms, although like any business you'll probably need a DBA certificate, tax ID, sales tax certification, and so on. For your own purposes, however, you'll need a written partnership agreement describing the arrangement.

Partnership Agreement Checklist

If you're setting up a partnership, it's essential to have a partnership agreement—a document that specifically states what's expected of both parties—so that there are as few ambiguities as possible. Be sure to include the following:

- Name of the partnership

- Where the business is to be located

- How much money each partner is to contribute

- Level of participation of each partner in profits and losses

- Salaries of partners

- How much each partner is to draw against profits

- Partners' responsibilities

- Noncompete agreements

- In the event of a dispute, whose decision will prevail

- How to admit new partners

- What happens if a partner retires or dies

- Accounting procedures (who signs checks, where the accounts are kept, who has access to the books)

- Procedures and causes for expulsion of partners

GSA BUSINESS SERVICE CENTERS

The General Services Administration oversees the purchase of about $10 billion in all kinds of goods and services for the federal government annually. Its Office of Economic Development also operates regional Small Business Centers to help you learn about opportunities that might exist for you to sell your product or service to the government, get copies of federal standards and specifications, study bidding histories, retrieve publications, and even receive business counseling. Call a regional center listed below to find your local contact.

New England	(607) 565-8100
Northeast	(212) 264-1234
Mid-Atlantic	(215) 656-5525
Southeast Sunbelt	(404) 331-5103
Great Lakes	(312) 353-5383
The Heartland	(816) 926-7203
Greater Southwest	(817) 978-3284
Rocky Mountain	(303) 236-7408
Pacific Rim	(415) 522-2700
S. CA Satellite	(213) 894-3210
Northwest/Arctic	(206) 931-7956
National Capitol	(202) 708-5804

While it's tempting to go into a partnership on a handshake alone, don't do it. Get a lawyer to help you draw up a partnership agreement detailing how profits and liabilities will be shared and how decisions will be made. Also describe any particular responsibilities each partner will have. And don't forget to include a way to end the agreement if the time comes.

A partnership caveat: Like any other piece of paper, a partnership agreement is only as good as the people behind it. Take extreme care in picking your partner. It's popular to take on a friend, relative, or even a spouse as a partner. If you do it, make sure your personal relationship isn't blinding you to that person's possible business failings—and vice versa. Don't take on as a partner a business powerhouse whom you personally can't stomach.

Partnerships are good because you can have a co-owner if your business needs special expertise, more capital, or another resource you can't supply on your own. Taxes are also easy. Any profits are taxed like a sole proprietor's, although you file a different form informing tax authorities of how the profits (or losses) are to be split up among the owner-partners.

It's somewhat easier to add partners and investors if you need additional expertise or more money. On the downside, there have to be at least two of you to have a partnership—no solos.

Like a sole owner, you're liable for making good on any debts incurred by the business. In

addition—and this is a major issue—you're liable for any contracts your partners sign or damage they cause. If you want to end the business, you may have trouble selling your share or otherwise getting out of the partnership if things don't work out.

Limited Partnership

A limited partnership is a business with two kinds of partners: general partners who manage the company and limited partners who contribute only capital. If the Compleat Pet were organized as a limited partnership, for instance, Ben and Mary would be the general partners while Hank would be a limited partner. In most other respects, including taxation, a limited partnership runs like a regular partnership.

The first major difference between general and limited partners has to do with liability. The general partners are liable for any debts the business produces. The limited partners' liabilities are limited to the capital invested in the business. Hank likes this part: If the business runs up a bill, he may lose his investment but creditors can't come after him for more. Secondly, while the general partner reaps the profits directly from the business, the limited partner's share of the profits comes in the form of dividends and distributions.

There's one problem with the limited partnership from Hank's perspective, however. Limited partners can take no role in running the business. If they do, they become general partners and are fully responsible for the business's debts. Since Hank wants to have some say in what goes on, this doesn't look like a good choice for him.

Where to Get Help with Choosing a Business Form

- *Your Secretary of State.* The Secretary of State of the state in which you are doing business will have forms, fee schedules, and other information that give you hard details to use in your decision. Check your phone book's blue government pages and look for "Secretary of State" under the listing for your state.

- *Small Business Administration.* The *Selecting the Legal Structure for Your Business* pamphlet is available for a nominal sum from the Small Business Administration, (800) 827-5722 or http://www.sba.gov

- *Internal Revenue Service.* Several IRS booklets are helpful, including *Tax Information on Partnerships* and similarly titled publications on corporations and S corporations. IRS: (800) 829-1040 or http://www.irs.gov

- *Trade Groups.* Industry associations, professional groups, and others may have experts available to talk to you about the best form for your business. To locate an appropriate trade association, look in the *Encyclopedia of Associations,* by Gale Research, (313) 961-2242 or (800) 877-4253.

- *The Professionals.* Your accountant and attorney are important stops along the way to choosing a business structure. Don't miss them.

PLAN, *plan,* and plan SOME MORE

CHAPTER SIX

Most businesses—even successful ones—are started without formal written business **plans.** *But having some-thing on paper can help with everything from raising start-up money to* **guiding you** *in times of trouble.*

You've already got a plan for how you expect your business to turn out, even if it's only a vague set of dreams in your head. That's great. Every business may not start with a plan, but it's safe to say that all of them start with a dream. Every small business expert worth his spreadsheet will tell you, however, that dreams are not enough—you need a written business plan.

If you press your small business expert long enough, she'll probably eventually admit that she didn't have a plan when she started her business. Or perhaps she'll say that, yes, she had one, but she hasn't laid eyes on it in years. If she didn't have one at all, she'll probably admit that she wished she had one and that she used it more often.

There is something to the conventional wisdom of plans. They may not solve every problem, but they'll give you a place to start and a focus as you build your business from the ground up.

There are actually several different kinds of business plans you need to consider doing. There is, of course, the formal business plan—the one you'll need to write if and when you decide to seek outside financing from a venture capitalist. That's the type of plan that intimidates most people. It's really not that hard, it just follows a specific format and contains very specific information. We'll give you the clues to putting one of those together later in this chapter. But first, you need to address the most important business plan—the one you write for yourself. Let's call it your business start-up plan.

One of the most valuable things your start-up plan will do is help you anticipate and think through future difficulties. Writing a start-up plan makes you sit down and answer all of the tough questions you need the answers to *before* you open the doors. Taking the time to answer them now just might save you a lot of anxious moments in the future. As you fill in the blanks, you'll have to ask—and answer—questions like: Who will be my main competition? Why should customers prefer me? And how quickly is this venture going to be profitable?

When you're doing your planning in your head, it's easy to forget about key details like that. But if you're leaving something out in your head planning, it will become glaringly apparent on paper. So make sure you write it down. Don't worry about the format or the language. Don't even worry about where you write it down, just do it. Then you'll always have something to refer to when you feel like things are off track.

A plan can also be a trusted adviser, keeping you focused during the inevitable tough, confusing times. Say a couple of years from now your venture is rolling along pretty well when one day you see what looks like another attractive opportunity. Only problem is, it is a completely different industry. Looking over your plan may convince you that you should stick to your knitting. Or, if the opportunity still looks like a winner after going through the same planning process you used in starting up your current venture, you may be able to charge ahead aggressively and confidently.

A good start-up plan can help you hire, train, and keep good employees by communicating to them your vision of how your company will grow. You know why you

think your business will succeed. But if you can't convince other people to join you in your belief, you'll have a hard time recruiting the crème de la crème of workers. A good plan can show skilled, in-demand people that you're serious and knowledgeable, and they'd do well to sign on. Once they are hired, a plan (or documents based on one) can help reinforce the values and goals you've chosen, and create a lasting corporate culture dedicated to achieving your dream.

Finally, if you're going to raise money from outside investors, a formal business plan is a flat necessity. But even if a relative or very close friend is going to give you money to start a business, you're going to have to show them what you plan to do with the money and how you plan to make your business a success. That, among other things, is exactly what a start-up plan does.

The Start-Up Approach

There's a way to create a helpful, appropriate business plan without investing too much time or setting yourself up for a fall.

First off, you have to decide if you're building a business as an entrepreneur or a free-lancer. An entrepreneur works to build a business bigger than herself, with significant financial business risks and numerous employees. A freelancer, on the other hand, is looking for the freedom and profit that come from being on your own, without the headaches that come from building a significant venture. Are you a graphic designer looking to go out on your own, a Big Six accountant looking to break away and start your own tax service, or an inventor with an idea for a new product and the dream of building a multimillion-dollar widget manufacturing company?

This is an important distinction when it comes to a business plan. Perhaps one business out of 1,000 gets external financing from a venture capitalist or a bank. The rest are self-funded by friends, family, and cash flow. If you're self-funded, you don't need a formal business plan. The format of the plan, in fact, can get you in a lot of trouble. Why? Because by focusing on the format, it's easy to avoid the really hard questions. The graphic designer and the accountant probably don't need to start with a formal plan, but the widget maker is going to need some serious financing.

Whether or not you intend to attract outside financing, you should create your start-up business plan first to help accomplish what you really need—a plan—before you have to wrestle with the formalities of pro formas, balance sheets, and the rest. Your start-up plan should actually consist of several miniplans, each one addressing a different aspect of your business.

The first business plan you should draw up is a one-page vision of next year and three years from now. Where will you be? How many employees will you have? What sorts of customers will you sell to? What will your reputation be? How much cash will you have in the bank? Focus on your goals. When you sit down and think about what kind of business you are trying to build, what comes to mind? Are you opening a pet supply store in a small town with the goal of breaking even in six months and making a modest living within a year? Are you starting a carpet cleaning store with the goal of owning five stores within five years?

If you can't get that on paper, it's time to stop and take a hard look at where you are and where you're going. Business guru Zig Ziglar tells the story of a plane that takes off from Dallas and heads for New York. After a few minutes, the wind has blown the plane a few miles off course. So the plane turns around and lands again in Dallas, getting ready for a new flight to New York.

Is that the way it really happens? Of course not! Instead, the pilot corrects his course, adjusts, and heads on a new path for New York. Your business is the same. If you know where you're going, it's going to be a lot easier to get there. But be flexible. Your plan isn't a prison. You can alter it as you go but at least it's a place to start.

The second plan to put together is the answer to the following question: What am I selling my customers that is worth buying? In other words, what are the specific benefits your product offers? Are they easy to replace? Are they really needed? Are you particularly qualified to offer them? You already answered a lot of these questions when you determined your positioning strategy. The key now is to define your product in relation to your position and make sure that they match.

This quickly segues into the second half of the question. Assuming you offer something that people want, how are you going to keep your competitors from offering the same thing, for less money? MBAs call that a barrier to entry. If you don't have

one, that's okay. (There are lots of businesses with few barriers, but it means you need to be prepared for competition and you can't expect unrealistic profits.)

The next plan that's critically important is a cash flow projection. By now, you've drawn up three or four mini-business plans so you have the idea. For this one, you need to write down how much money you're going to have in the bank at the end of every month. Do this by estimating how much you will spend (in checks or cash) in the month and how much you will receive (in checks or cash) every month. If the total amount of money is ever less than zero, you lose. Boom. So the alert entrepreneur has a very good idea of exactly what's going on with his cash.

Don't even start a business unless your cash flow projection shows you can make it at least nine months without running out of money. For some businesses, a two-year reserve is better. Here are 25 costs many businesses will incur in the first few months of life. Your business may not have all. It may have others not on the list. Think expansively on this topic. Try to identify every cost or potential cost you could incur, and plan for them. Common ones are:

- Accounting fees

- Advertising

- Bad debts

- Building or rent

- Cleaning and maintenance

- Contingency fund

- Decorating

- Entertainment and meals

- Equipment

- Furniture

- Income tax withholding

LOW-COST BUSINESS PLANS

Check out the SBA resources for developing a business plan inexpensively.

Small Business
Development Center
Program
Small Business
Administration
409 Third St. SW
Washington, DC 20024
SBA Answer Desk:
(800) 827-5722
Web site:
http://www.sba.gov

SCORE
Small Business
Administration
409 Third St. SW
Washington, DC 20024
(202) 205-6762
Web site:
http://www.score.org

- Insurance

- Interest on loans

- Inventory

- Leasehold improvements

- Legal fees

- Postage

- Salaries and benefits

- Sales tax withholding

- Shipping

- Stationery

- Supplies

- Travel costs

- Utility deposits

The last miniplan to do is a marketing plan. Once again, you get the ball rolling by asking yourself a series of questions: How are you going to convey your position in the marketplace to your customers? What ads are you going to run? How often? How will you measure them? Here's where you choose the tools you are going to use to reach your target market.

Check out chapter nine for a host of marketing techniques you can employ. Then make a list of the ten methods that you think will work best for you.

Use the worksheet below as a model for your marketing plan. Fill it out for a six-month period. At the end of that six months, fill it out again.

Here's an example of the marketing worksheet filled out by the owner of a pet supply store mentioned above. It outlines the top ten promotional and advertising tools the owner plans to use.

Tool	Cost Per Use		Frequency	Monthly Cost	Total Cost
Pennysaver ad	$300		1x per month	$300	$1,800
Bag flyers	.02	per flyer	125 per week	10	60
Chamber mtgs.	50	per year	1x per month	4	25
Yellow Pages ad	500		1x per year	42	250
Annual Pet Beauty Show promotion with local paper					250
Annual sponsorship of two Little League baseball teams					100
Semi-annual Stock-Up sale and carnival					0
Free rabies shots offered to all customers (comarket with vet)					0
Frequent Customer Card (buy nine food bags, get one free)					$12 per bag of free food awarded

The Formal Plan

Despite the touted advantages of plans, it's a fact that most businesses are started without plans. That includes some of the most successful enterprises of the era.

Scott McNealy, cofounder of Sun Microsystems, glanced at a plan his partners wrote immediately after starting the company. Then McNealy (an MBA, by the way) filed it away and never looked at it again. Meanwhile, Sun grew to be a multibillion-dollar company.

An even bigger computer company, Digital Equipment, received its start-up funding from investors who were convinced to back the fledgling venture by a plan that cofounder Ken Olsen later admitted was copied almost verbatim from a college economics textbook. Only the company's name and financial data were changed.

Preparing a business plan may sometimes actually be riskier than going without one. A plan predicts the future and so, according to Yogi Berra, is risky. It won't help you much if you use bad information to prepare it, don't share it with others, don't update it, and don't ever consult it yourself. It could even be a mistake to prepare a plan if you spend too much time on it or take it to be an infallible predictor.

Elements of a Business Plan

You learned earlier that making a business plan is a little like filling in the blanks of a form, and most do follow a general basic format and have many features in common. As a rule, every plan will have at minimum an executive summary, a description of your product or service, a description of your business and industry, and separate sections covering your management team, marketing strategy, and financial information.

Within these broad parameters, however, each plan is likely to be unique. That's because different factors are important for different companies and different industries. For instance, a plan for a computer retail store may need a separate section on location. A plan for an import-export trader might briefly mention location, but have a whole section on shipping.

Don't be a prisoner of format. Whatever is crucial to your company, cover it in the plan. Whatever's not, minimize it or skip it completely. You can use the following detailed descriptions of common business plan elements to guide you in creating the individual elements of your own plan.

Your Executive Summary

This is a one- or two-page snapshot of what you're up to. The aim of the executive summary is to give a reader a concise understanding of the basic concept and highlights of your plan.

The summary usually takes the form of a synopsis of the various elements of the plan (more on those in a minute). Together, these short takes should convince the reader your business makes sense, it's been thoroughly planned, you can run it, people will

buy what you're selling, you can beat your competition, your financial projections are reasonable, and, if you're seeking investors, they'll earn a fair profit without undue risk.

Just because it's short, don't underestimate the importance of the summary. It may be the only part of your plan anybody reads. It is almost certain to be the first part they read. Because it's so vital to coherently sum up the rest of your plan here, make it the last part of your plan you write.

Here's a tip. If you have an especially dramatic or interesting story to tell about how your company was founded, try a narrative approach to your executive summary instead of a straight synopsis of your plan's sections. Bernard Salick was motivated to start what became a nationwide chain of cancer treatment centers after his six-year-old daughter was diagnosed with bone cancer. Telling a story like that will make your summary more readable and, possibly, compelling.

Description of Your Product or Service

Every business is founded on a product or service that is sold to someone who chooses it over something else. What is your product or service? What makes it worthwhile? Who's going to buy it and why? (Since most entrepreneurs have pretty strong feelings about their product or service, you're probably going to really enjoy writing this section. Let your conviction show.)

SAMPLE EXECUTIVE SUMMARY

Authentic Bagel Shop will be a gourmet coffee and bagel bar catering to breakfast, lunch, and take-out customers.

It will occupy a 1,200-square-foot space in the Westwinds Shopping Center in the town of Smithburg. The location is near the intersection of the turnpike and Main Street and on the route many residents take to work at the glass plant.

Costs will be minimized due to the fact that the location has been empty for three months, and that the fixtures of a failed bagel store were purchased at a substantial discount. This will allow Authentic Bagel to invest in the highest-quality ingredients and obtain premium prices.

The owner of Authentic Bagel, John True, has ten years experience in the retail bakery and restaurant business.

SAMPLE DESCRIPTION OF YOUR PRODUCT OR SERVICE

Past Perfect Antiques will offer fine European antiques from sources in England, Spain, France, and Denmark. The emphasis will be on country furniture from the nineteenth century, and on pieces that are both affordable and distinctive.

The product description has one must-do. It must make clear what is unique or special about your offering. Emphasize the new value that you bring to the market. You may want to include photographs or drawings of a product or a detailed description of a service you'll provide, stressing the ways in which what you're selling will add value for buyers. When Jeff Bezos raised $8 million to launch Amazon.com, an online bookstore, he got investors' attention by stating that his online shoppers would be able to browse 1.1 million book titles, compared to 300,000 for an average big bookstore.

Many product and service categories are crowded and distinctions between different companies' offerings may be hard for novices to grasp. Help your plan's readers see how you're better by preparing a table or matrix precisely comparing your features to others. Check out computer or car magazines or *Consumer Reports* for examples of how to do it effectively.

Description of Your Business and Industry

Products don't succeed on their own. Even great ones have to have good businesses behind them. This is the place to describe some of the details about your business. When was it founded? Who owns it? Is it a sole proprietorship, partnership, corporation, or other form (see chapter five)? How will your product or service be designed, produced, and distributed?

Don't stop with a description of your business as it exists today. Loudly state your goals for the future. Be specific. If you think you can become "the largest auto detailer in the Tri-Cities," say so. If you hope to someday snare 5 percent of the market for planning incentive travel programs for the insurance industry, share the news.

End this section with a one-paragraph summary of your business's most important strengths and weaknesses. You'll be going over these highlights frequently in this plan, but you can't do it too often.

Your Management Team

Time and again, you'll hear business owners say that people are their most valuable assets. Be sure to describe these assets in your own business plan. Who are your key employees? What does each do? How do they work together?

A lot of people are starting companies alone. But you shouldn't skip this section because of that. If you're the only person who'll be working for your company, fine. Tell about yourself and your credentials for starting this business. Don't overinflate your C.V., of course. But, on the other hand, never ever apologize for not having some particular credential or experience.

If you've assembled a sizable group of partners or employees to help you, you don't have to describe each and every one. Focus in particular on the central players in your management team: marketing, financial, production, and administration. If your company has special nonmanagement key players, such as a technology guru responsible for developing and refining new products, be sure to describe them here as well.

For a complex, sizable business, include an organizational chart to give a visual grasp of the chain of command and the various players' responsibilities. If your key employees are highly experienced, you can include brief résumés of their careers in this section.

SAMPLE DESCRIPTION OF YOUR BUSINESS AND INDUSTRY

Most of Clean Sweep Maid Service's customers will be two-income families in the upscale community of Wind Hill. They will require bonded employees, environmentally friendly cleansers, and reasonable, but not the lowest, prices. Clean Sweep will be the only cleaning service targeting the growing, affluent neighborhood of Wind Hill.

Your Marketing Strategy

The old saw about inventing a better mousetrap and the world beating a path to your door probably isn't true anymore, if it ever was. You have to have a solid marketing strategy to have a hope of selling a single mousetrap of any kind. In this section, you'll answer people who may be wondering: How are you going to promote, price, and place your product or service? And why are you doing it that way?

SAMPLE MANAGEMENT TEAM

Busy Books will be managed by its owner, Edward Teague, who has five years' experience as manager of a national book chain location in the nearby regional shopping mall. Mr. Teague has a degree in business administration from the University of Southern California. He will be assisted by his wife, Sally, who graduated from USC with an English degree.

In this section you'll outline your advertising plans. Where are you going to advertise? How often? What's your budget for ads? You'll also describe public relations efforts, cooperative giveaways, and other promotions. You may not want to offer too many details here—business plan readers don't need to know the headlines of press releases you'll send out announcing your new mousetrap, or how many ad insertions you plan for *Mouser's Monthly*. Just make sure you have thought it all through carefully and provide enough minutiae to convey that impression.

Pricing is a key element in any offering. What are you going to charge? What makes you think consumers will pay it? Do you have any flexibility about raising or lowering prices? This section should answer these questions. Be as precise as possible. Say, "We'll sell our trap for $9 wholesale, with a suggested retail price of $18, placing it in the middle of the industry pricing scheme," instead of vaguely promising you can make them for 10 percent less than competitors, with features that will let you sell them for 10 percent more.

Once you price it and promote it, you've got to place it. Most small businesses fill only one role in the distribution chain. Are you going to sell to end users? Retailers? Wholesalers? If you're relying on others to do part of the job, how will your products

reach buyers? Michael Dell founded Dell Computer and grew it to billions of dollars in sales on the strength of what was then a new idea: Sell personal computers directly to end users through the mail and telephone orders. Many successful companies are likewise founded on a new manner of distribution. Make sure yours is outlined here.

One of the best things any business plan can have is solid market research that describes a large, unmet need. Identify prospective customers who are likely to buy what you're selling, and you're a long way toward crafting a helpful plan. Don't skimp on selected important details.

When Mike and Pam Henricks were planning to start a Texas veterinary hospital, Mike dug up information on the income, number of pets owned, and other relevant information on households within a several-mile radius of their planned location. He used the U.S. Census Bureau, the city economic development department, the local chamber of commerce, and the veterinarian association to cull this data. Along with other information about competitive vets in their service area, this provided a clear idea of whether they were serving an unmet need.

You don't have to spend a fortune for useful market research. Two entrepreneurs getting ready to start an office supply wholesaler got the basic information they needed about their prospective market's size by simply looking through corporate directories for companies in their area with sales of $50 million or more. Corporate directories are available for you to study for free at many public libraries.

SAMPLE MARKETING STRATEGY

Butler Communications plans to budget 12 percent of sales to marketing, including:

• Publicity mailings of sample premier issues of *Cigar Collector's Newsletter* to 100 local and national media outlets

• Quarter-page advertisements in four wine and cigar magazines, on a rotating basis

• Regular mailings of sample issues to 25 cigar and wine editors, producers, and other media people

• Travel expenses to send the editor and publisher to four trade shows and cigar conventions each year

Financial Information

Profit is the main reason for most businesses' existence, and in this section of your plan, you'll need to show how you expect your business to perform. At minimum, you'll need cash flow forecasts and income projections and perhaps other financial information, like a detailed analysis of your fixed and variable expenses or a breakeven analysis that will let your potential investors know how much you'll need to sell before you start making a profit.

This section is likely to be mostly tables, with some text footnotes. The tables will cover your profit and loss projections, cash flow projections, and balance sheets. You'll also need to provide income statements showing your estimated profit and loss for each quarter for the next two years. You may want to also give annual projections for the next five years.

Don't be afraid of going into too much detail, especially when it comes to spotting costs. You should have separate line items for any significant expenses. Some entrepreneurs go even further. Barbara Bissett, president of Bissett Steel, a 19-employee Ohio steel distributor, says, "On our statements I have a policy of no miscellaneous categories. If it's got a cost, it's got a name."

Use your best, most realistic estimates of sales and expenses to come up with these projections. You have to assume some things, but don't assume that anybody reading your plan will make the same assumptions. Use text footnotes to your table to explain your assumptions.

Cash flow should be detailed quarterly for at least a couple of years. If you expect to be running on razor-thin cash levels for awhile, you may want to even have monthly cash flow projections for several months. Be conservative when forecasting cash flow; it's easy to find uses for extra money, but if you run short for even a month it could mean an untimely end for your venture.

Balance sheets show your assets and liabilities and compare them to come up with a net worth for your business. Assets include things like money in the bank, receivables from customers, inventory, fixtures and equipment and, possibly, valuable trademarks or patents. Liabilities are bills for supplies and utilities and other stuff you have yet to pay, taxes you owe, and loans you are paying off. The difference between them is your business's net worth.

Unlike cash flow and income statements, which cover periods of time such as a year or a quarter, balance sheets are like snapshots showing where you stand on a single day, usually the end of the fiscal year. For that reason, you may want to prepare a couple of balance sheets, one for when you start your business and one projecting where you'll stand after the first year.

Everybody knows you're guessing when you make projections. You can give your guesses more credibility if you prepare three sets. One should be a conservative forecast representing 50 percent of the sales volume you really expect. Another should be 100 percent of realistically expected sales. Finally, prepare an optimistic version showing what would happen if sales hit 150 percent, or even 200 percent, of the middle projection.

Appendixes

You should probably create a separate section for any special issues you feel are highly important for your business. For instance, if you are going to start a boutique selling authentic African art, the question of where you are going to buy your inventory may warrant individual treatment. If you want to include other material that doesn't seem to fit anywhere else, but doesn't justify a separate headline, you can have an appendix.

An appendix at the end of your plan may be a good place to display photos of your product, advertising samples, press clippings, or testimonials. Take care not to stick anything critical back there where it might be missed, however.

How Long Should Your Plan Be?

If all you're trying to do is create a plan for your personal use, you may need no more than the back of an envelope to jot down key points to jog your memory. That's especially true if you are still a good ways from actually starting your business, and if you plan a small, perhaps one-person enterprise requiring no outside funding.

SBA BUSINESS PLANNING ONLINE

If you're going to be doing an informal business plan, there is a great online resource. You can get to it on the Internet from the SBA Web site at http://www.sba.gov. Click on Starting Your Business and you'll find a link to Developing Your Business Plan Workshop. The workshop will take you through the steps of creating a business plan by showing you an outline and telling you how to fill in the spaces. If you're going to be using a business plan as a tool for getting financing, you should probably get some human professional help, but if your objective is to have a concrete plan to keep your goals and numbers straight, this may be all you need.

The opposite case is that of a business that is either under way or will be very shortly, that is of substantial size, and that is seeking financing. A plan like this may run anywhere from 10 to 100 pages or more, with the shorter plans sufficing for small, new operations and the longer ones for older, bigger enterprises.

Forty pages is a sensible length limit for almost any business plan. If you have complex technology, legal issues, or other business matters that take space to explain, you may want to go longer.

Before you write a really long plan, keep this in mind: You want people to actually read this plan, not flip through it in boredom or frustration. And this is a good opportunity to show you can be efficient and organized. Use it.

Sources for More Info

It's always a good idea to look at some sample business plans before getting started. That will help you better visualize what your plan should contain and what it should look like. There are many sources for more information on business plans.

- *The Entrepreneur & Small Business Problem Solver: An Encyclopedic and Reference Guide* by William A. Cohen, published by John Wiley & Sons, 1990. This comprehensive small business guidebook includes a section on business plans along with advice on raising money, business law, buying insurance, leasing equipment, financial management, and more.

- *The Successful Business Plan: Secrets & Strategies* by Rhonda M. Abrams, published by Oasis Press, 1993. This in-depth book on planning includes dozens of worksheets, special planning considerations for various types of businesses and whole chapters on everything from writing a cover letter for prospective investors to tips on shaving time from the planning process.

- *The Business Planning Guide: Creating a Plan for Success in Your Own Business* by David H. Bangs Jr., published by Upstart Publishing, 1996. A 150-page manual on writing a business plan tailored to your specific business. Includes worksheets and checklists.

- *Anatomy of a Business Plan: A Step-By-Step Guide to Starting Smart, Building the Business and Securing Your Company's Future* by Linda Pinson and Jerry Jinnett, published by Upstart Publishing, 1996.

- *BizPlanBuilder Interactive,* by JIAN USA, (800) 346-5426. This software for PCs and Macintoshes leads you through a step-by-step process to create a plan. It contains 90 typed pages of example text and what-if scenarios to fine-tune forecasts.

- *PlanMaker,* by POWERSolutions for Business, (800) 955-3337. This software for Macs and PCs uses in-depth questionnaires to help you assemble and input appropriate information, tailor your financial statements to meet investors' needs, and format it all into a professional-looking document.

Throughout this chapter, there are sidebars with short examples of the Executive Summary and other sections of a formal business plan. They are good examples, but are a bit artificial in the sense that a typical business plan can be 50 to 100 pages long. Turn to the appendix at the end of this book for some longer examples from a few real-life business plans.

SECURING the financing you may need now OR LATER

CHAPTER SEVEN

*It takes money to make money. You may need to **raise money** to start your business now or to grow it later on.*

If you're opening a bakery, you have to rent space, buy ovens, and lay in bags of flour and other raw materials long before you ever ring up your first sale. If you're a one-person home-based bookkeeping service, you're going to need a computer, desk, and phone line (in addition to a green eyeshade, of course) to ply your trade.

All that stuff costs money, and it's one reason people say you need money to make money. Start-ups need money to pay for everything from stationery to inventory before they can even open their doors. You may also need financing to pay for growth later. If you're a manufacturer, you may need to buy new product machines, or pay for raw materials to turn into finished products to fulfill new or expected orders.

Financing is what you do when you don't have the money you need to get started or to grow later on. There are different kinds of financing, including debt and equity, and there are lots of places to get it, from your own piggy bank to your neighborhood bank and even, conceivably, a public stock offering on Wall Street.

Here's a caveat: You should definitely read this section, but not every business needs significant financing. William Hewlett and David Packard pooled just $438 in savings to start the company that became Hewlett-Packard, with annual sales today of more than $25 billion. Some start-ups can be gotten off the ground for lunch money, literally, $10 or less. You can start a lawn care service, petsitting service, or other small service enterprise, for example, by photocopying a hundred flyers and posting them on bulletin boards in your town. And once they're up and going, many businesses finance their growth with no financing beyond start-up capital, generating profits from sales to pay for everything they need.

So, How Much Do You Need?

You'll likely have two different kinds of financing needs. The first is start-up capital, to allow you to open your doors. The second is growth capital, to allow you to purchase goods for manufacturing or resale, open new offices, and the like.

First things first, figure out your start-up cash needs. You can get a ballpark estimate of start-up financing needs by looking at what it cost other people to get businesses like yours off the ground. One study of four broad types of businesses found wide variations.

- Service firms are cheapest. Two out of four service firms are started with under $10,000, and nearly three-quarters get under way with less than $50,000 in start-up capital.

- Retail/wholesale operations have the next-lowest start-up needs. About one in five begins with under $10,000, and two-thirds take less than $50,000.

- Financial and "other" types of businesses are more expensive, but almost half begin with less than $50,000.

- Manufacturers and high-tech firms have the biggest start-up tab. More than four out of five need over $50,000 to get going.

Individual businesses are likely to have cash needs that go way outside these categories. So while a computer software developer started up for $25,000, a new real estate magazine took $95,000, a diaper manufacturing company absorbed $75,000, and a maker of cigarette machines went through $2.1 million.

Of course, your business isn't quite like any other. So use these group averages and specific examples as merely indicators. To do much more than guess at how much you'll need, you'll have to do some careful analysis of your cash needs.

Here's an example of a worksheet that was used for figuring what it would take to start a women's clothing store and stay open for three months:

Preopening Expenses	
Opening inventory	$30,000
Furniture and fixtures (down payment)	4,000
Accounting, legal, license, and other fees	3,000
Utility, rent and other deposits	3,000
Ongoing Expenses	
Payroll (first three months)	6,000
Rent (first three months)	4,500
Advertising (first three months)	3,000
TOTAL START-UP CAPITAL	$53,500

Different businesses have different amounts for these categories. If you're planning a big, warehouse-style store, you might require much larger figures for inventory. Are you locating in a high-traffic space at an upscale mall? Plug in higher rent. And if you expect to attract customers by offering extended hours or attentive personal service, expect higher labor costs.

Other firms have completely different categories. A manufacturer would have expenses for production equipment, for example. A marketing consultant setting up shop for the first time would have no inventory and probably little or no advertising cost. However, her travel budget could be sizable. And if she expected it would take quite a while to land her first client, she might include six months' or even a year's worth of rent and other ongoing expenses in her start-up cost estimate.

Other common start-up outlays include the cost of remodeling or redecorating the space in which you'll conduct your business, the cost of moving equipment or inventory to the new location, and—last but not least—a contingency fund to cover emergencies.

How Much Can You Get?

How much you need is one thing. How much you can get is another. They are, however, related. Odds are you won't be able to get more financing than you can show you need, but you should definitely try. It's a lot harder to secure more financing if you run out of cash the first time. An estimate of start-up capital requirements that shows careful information gathering and rigorous analysis can convince a reluctant banker that you deserve what you're asking for.

An equally important figure in determining your financing capability is your company's net book value, or net worth. At its simplest, your net value is what's left after you take your company's assets (inventory, receivables, cash on hand) and subtract its liabilities (money you owe for taxes, loans, supplier credit, and the like). That figure tells the

TRY IT HIS WAY

When you're looking for start-up capital, you need to do everything possible to convince potential investors you're really passionate about your venture—even if it means quitting your job before your business is up and running. Michael Damphousse of Pangaea Consulting, a software company, found this out the hard way. Although he had approached investors with the concept for his new software venture, it wasn't until he had quit his position as head of marketing for AEG Schneider Automation that backers felt he was truly committed to Pangaea. It was then that they coughed up the $150,000 he needed to get his fledgling enterprise off the ground.

banker how much he can figure on recouping if you go bust because he'll get to claim all of your assets if you default on his loan.

Here's a sample net worth statement for a small bicycle pump manufacturer.

Assets	
Cash	$ 6,050
Receivables	10,550
Inventory	6,700
Real estate	65,000
Machinery & equipment	24,200
Other assets	4,500
Total assets	$ 117,000

Liabilities	
Bank loans	$ 28,500
Accounts payable	4,200
Other liabilities	2,500
Mortgage	50,750
Total liabilities	$ 85,950

NET WORTH	$ 31,050

Your company's value is not the only net worth figure a banker or other lender is likely to be interested in. Since you're just starting out, you will probably be asked to personally guarantee any loans you take out, backing them with any personal assets you have, like your house or any investments you may own. For this, you'll need to fill out an individual net worth statement similar to what you complete to apply for a home mortgage or car loan.

You might also need to prepare a cash flow projection if you're applying for a loan. The idea here is to show that you'll have the cash on hand to make the required loan payments on time and in full.

Kinds of Financing

There are two main kinds of financing: debt and equity. Both can provide cash to start your business. But you'll still want to choose carefully which you try to secure. Start by getting a clue about the main differences between them.

Debt financing means borrowing money. Like any other loan, you have to pay back the money, with interest. If you borrow money and can't pay it back, your company—and possibly you—may be forced into bankruptcy. The lender doesn't own any of the company, gets no share of the profits or losses, and can't tell you how to run it. Borrowing doesn't affect your ownership of the company.

Equity financing involves selling pieces of ownership in your company in exchange for money to start up or expand. You don't have to pay back money received for an equity share, nor do you have to pay interest on it. That doesn't mean equity financing is without cost, however. An equity investor is an owner, sharing in profits and losses, and is entitled to some say in running the company. The more of your company's equity you sell, the less of the company you own. If you sell too much of your company for equity, it becomes someone else's business.

Each kind of financing has pluses and minuses. Which should you go for? It depends on where you are, where you're going, and how you want to get there. It's often very difficult for a brand-new company to get debt financing, for instance. Equity investors tend to be more willing to take risks with start-ups, because they know that if your company is successful, they'll make money too. Banks don't care about how successful you are. They'll just want their money back with interest. Many companies choose both debt and equity, raising some capital with loans and other money by selling equity.

TRY IT HIS WAY

Tom Stemberg is the founder, chairman, and CEO of Staples, the office supply megastore. In the first few months of doing business, he says, Staples just seemed to eat cash instead of spitting it out the way the company does these days. What got him through that critical period was that the $4.5 million in venture capital he raised was really more money than he needed. Don't let insufficient start-up capital kill your dream—get more than you need.

Use the Basic Rule of Finance to help decide what kind of financing to seek. It says you should match the financing you seek to the way you plan to use the money. If you need money in the short-term in order to buy inventory you'll be selling within a few months, go for the debt financing such as a bank loan first. You'll be able to pay it back after you sell the inventory, and you need the money for a very specific purpose and time period. If you need to raise cash to fund a long-term research and development project, on the other hand, consider some equity financing. You'll need some investment-minded capitalists behind you in order to develop your business over the long haul.

Sources of Money

"Can anybody remember when the times were not hard, and money not scarce?" Ralph Waldo Emerson said that. But the fact is, hard times or not, there are lots of places to get money. A fairly comprehensive list would include personal savings, partners, employees, friends and relatives, customers, suppliers, banks, credit cards, a Small Business Administration loan, a Small Business Investment Company, community development corporations, asset-based lenders, private stock placements, angels, corporate investors, joint ventures, venture capital, initial public offering of stock, Small Company Offering Registration, and corporate bonds.

None of these sources is perfect for every business. Each has its own pluses, minuses, limits, risks, and costs.

Personal Savings

Personal savings are the most popular form of start-up financing. A study by the National Federation of Independent Businesses found nearly half of all start-ups are funded primarily with the savings of the founder or founders. In fact, chances are slim you'll be able to start a business without putting in any of your own cash. Other investors like to see a founder who believes in the business, and what better way to demonstrate your belief than by putting your own money behind it?

Using personal savings has several advantages. You decide how much to invest, when to invest, and, if things go badly, when to pull out. You don't have to pay it back or

SAVE A DOLLAR TO RAISE A DOLLAR

The best way to raise money is to cut expenses. When negotiating your rent or purchasing your equipment, don't think like a consumer. Think like a businessowner who has to protect her cash at all costs. Try to negotiate a lease that allows you to pay less rent upfront and for the first six months, and more rent after you're up and running. Try leasing equipment instead of purchasing it outright. You'll have to pay interest, but at least you won't have to lay out as much cash. Your cash is your most important asset. Guard it!

pay interest. You retain personal control and get to keep all the profits (unless you bring in other equity investors).

The main downside of relying on personal savings is that you may not have enough—or be willing to risk enough—to get the business up and going. Using other sources of financing increases the amount you have to spend and spreads the risk.

Partners

Entrepreneurs join forces as partners to pool resources, including money. If you don't have enough cash to get your business off the ground, you can take on a partner. The downside of taking on a partner is that you lose total ownership and control. The upside is, you get an associate who is committed to seeing the venture succeed. It can be a powerful combo. To raise $1,300 to start Apple Computer, Steve Jobs sold his Volkswagen and Steve Wozniak sold his calculator. Jobs also provided the marketing charisma, while The Woz was the engineer.

Employees

Your employees have a big stake in your company's success and a lot of built-in knowledge about what that's going to require. Since you can't raise cash from employees until you have some, this funding source is more for businesses with somewhat of a track record than for a start-up. But if you require funds down the road, don't forget to look inside your company for loans and equity capital.

Friends and Relatives

About one in eight businesses is started with loans or investments from friends and relatives. Like employees, friends and family already want you to succeed. The risk is that you may damage personal relationships if the business doesn't succeed. To reduce that risk, explain clearly how and when loans will be repaid and with what interest rate, if applicable. For equity investors, everyone should understand what role they will play, under what conditions you can buy back their interest, and how profits and losses will be shared. Finally, put everything in writing. This will help reduce misunderstandings.

FINANCING RULE OF THUMB

Always try to get more money than you need the first time around. It's always more difficult to secure financing if you come up short.

Customers

A trio of hot air balloonists used savings to make a prototype of their design for a new type of balloon, then asked buyers for 50 percent down payments for orders. They used the down payments to finance purchase of machinery and materials to build the first production units. This probably won't work if, say, you're opening a dry cleaner. But you may be able to do something similar if you plan to offer a truly unique service or product, especially if it has a high value to your customers.

Suppliers

Suppliers are a much more likely source of start-up financing. If you're starting a restaurant, for example, one of your major start-up costs is going to be purchasing food. Normal terms for restaurant supplies are 30 days. If you can get your suppliers to sell you on credit enough ingredients to get you through the first 90 days, you're three times closer to your first blue-plate special.

Banks

A commercial bank is the first place many people think of when they're seeking financing. And banks or other institutional lenders do fund nearly a third of start-ups (through loans; banks are rarely equity investors). To use this convenient and widely available source of cash, you need to understand the Four Cs: Character, Capacity, Capital, and Collateral. These criteria are used by all bankers to decide whether to loan you money. If you can satisfy the Four Cs, you're likely to get your loan. The formal business plan we described in chapter six is the best tool you have to convince a bank to loan you some dough. Here's what they're looking for:

- *Character.* Your banker wants to look inside your heart (by looking at your credit history) to see if you are inclined to pay your bills. He or she will check with your past creditors, suppliers, and others to see how your character measures up.

- *Capacity.* Here your banker is asking: Will your company generate enough cash flow to make the payments? And do you have the management ability to run the company?

- *Capital.* It's usually not enough to project cash flows sufficient to pay back a loan. A banker wants to see capital (cash and resources like investment or money market accounts) on your company's balance sheet sufficient to keep it going, and keep loan payments coming, if profits dry up for some reason.

- *Collateral.* You're likely to have to back up your debt with something of value the banker can take if you fail to pay it back. A pizza restaurant entrepreneur may have to promise her ovens; an interior decorator may have to promise his office furnishings. Whatever it is, it must be easy to sell and valuable enough to cover the amount of the debt.

Are the Four Cs all you need? Not quite. You may also have to show that you have adequate insurance coverage, favorable economic trends, and weak rivals. One thing bankers really like is a lot of personal investment. The more money you have at stake in the business, the easier it will be to raise more.

There are a couple of different kinds of credit you can get from a bank. First of all, a bank may loan you a designated sum for a preset purpose, such as $20,000 to buy a new delivery car. You'll usually have to start making payments soon after you secure financing on this kind of loan, and pay it off after a set period of time ranging from a few months to a year or more.

A line of credit lets you borrow money as you need it up to a set amount without having to apply for a new loan every time. You have more flexibility about how you use the proceeds of a line of credit. Credit lines are usually revolving, like a credit card. That is, you don't have to ever pay it off completely, as long as you make the interest payments and pay down the principal if you ever get above the limit.

Credit Cards

You have only to check your mailbox to know that even if nobody else will lend you money, credit card companies will. Credit cards are intended to help consumers buy couches, not finance start-ups. They carry high interest rates, low credit limits (for a business) and require relatively rapid payback. However, many shoestring operations get started on credit cards, then move up to more conventional (and cheaper) forms of financing. It can take surprisingly little. A corporate refugee who wanted to start his own software company raised $11,000 by maxing out a couple of gold cards. That financed development of his first program, and the sales of that paid for later ones.

Small Business Administration Loans

Although it's rare, the SBA can make you a loan directly. More likely it will guarantee a loan made by another institution, such as a bank. SBA loans are attractive because they offer lower-than-usual interest rates. You can also take longer to pay back an SBA loan than most other business loans. The SBA uses many of the same guidelines as other lenders, but its role is specifically to act as lender of last resort. If everybody else turns you down, you can at least get a hearing here. However, fewer than 1 percent of start-ups are actually financed by the government. And even if you get the money, it may take months to navigate the inevitable bureaucracy.

The Supporting Players: Documents to Submit with a Loan Application

When you apply for a business loan, you'll need to provide evidence of collateral that you own personally and/or that the business owns. Personal collateral includes real estate deeds, savings account statements or passbooks, bonds, certificates of deposit, and securities. Business collateral includes accounts receivable, inventory, equipment and machinery, contracts receivable, and real estate.

In addition to the loan application, you'll need to supply:
• Current financial statement

• Income tax returns for the last three years

• Cash flow projections

• Partnership agreement or articles of incorporation

• Estimates of equipment purchases

• Résumé

• Itemization of personal debt (lenders' names and addresses, account numbers, terms, amounts)

Small Business Investment Companies

SBICs are private enterprises licensed by the SBA to fund start-ups. They are, however, able to be more flexible about providing both debt and equity financing. Some specialize in agricultural, aerospace, or other industries. The SBA can provide you with a list of nearby SBICs.

Asset-Based Lenders

An asset-based loan is a loan secured by the value of an asset. A printer, say, borrows to buy a printing press and pledges to give the bank that press if he can't make the payments. You can also finance other assets such as accounts receivable or inventory through one of two methods known as factors and floor planning.

Factors are specialized financiers most closely associated with the garment industry but now widely used in other industries as well. You can find one by looking in the business-to-business phone book under "factors." In factoring, a firm sells its accounts receivable to the factor. The factor collects the accounts receivable, keeping the difference between what he paid the merchant and what he can collect. Factors purchase your accounts receivable at a discount to their face value. Since most start-ups don't have any accounts receivable, this is usually a method of financing for better established firms.

Floor planning is a way to finance inventory based on the credit of the vendor, as well as your own credit. The lender owns your inventory until it's sold. In the auto dealership industry, lenders making what are known there as flooring loans retain title to the cars on the dealer's lot until consumers buy them. Similar loans known as "warehouse receipt" loans are common in agriculture. The lender has title to the inventory, such as a grain elevator, held in trust by a third party.

Private Stock Placements

If you're a corporation, you can sell stock to a limited pool of investors in a private stock placement. This is a way to raise capital without having to offer equity in your

company to the entire public. You offer equity in your company to a limited number of potential investors. A limited pool doesn't mean a limited future—Ford Motor had just 11 investors in the private stock placement that financed its start-up in 1903.

Private stock placements are cheaper than borrowing money—remember that with equity financing you don't have to pay investors back or pay interest. But you do lose some control. If you sell a majority share, you may lose practically all control. If your business is successful after a few years, you may be able to buy out your start-up investors. Or you may be able to find so-called silent partners, frequently friends or relatives who buy stock and take ownership, but not any role in running the business.

Angels

Business angels can be heavenly. These private investors back companies that are too new, too unproven, or too unpromising to attract other investors such as venture capitalists. Usually, angels are friends, relatives, or colleagues. Successful entrepreneurs, especially retired ones, are especially likely to become angels. Angels may be able to invest considerable money in your venture without requiring the kind of documentation that other investors do. But, particularly if you're dealing with a relative or friend, do put your arrangement in writing to reduce misunderstandings.

HOW MUCH IS ENOUGH?

Keep in mind that it could be some time before your fledgling business realizes a profit—so make sure you get sufficient start-up capital to keep it running during that initial phase. The SBA advises that you should have enough cash to cover operating expenses for at least a year to avoid being one of those sad statistics of new business failures.

Corporate Investors

If you've got a promising technology, a one-of-a-kind location, or a particular service that a large company is interested in, you may be able to get that company to invest in you. Many entrepreneurs have been financed by former employers who liked the business idea well enough to back it, but didn't want to do it internally. One engineer spent five years trying unsuccessfully to convince

Are You Eligible for an SBA Loan?

To be eligible for an SBA loan, you must have been denied a conventional loan by a private lender. In addition, you must meet SBA's criteria as a "small business," which—good news—applies to about 90 percent of U.S. businesses. Your business must also be:

• For profit

• Independently owned and operated

• Not the dominant player in its field

Here are some types of businesses that are NOT eligible:
• Consumer and marketing co-ops

• Cable TV systems that broadcast live stations

• Academic schools (with the exception of preschools and kindergartens as long as they are not primarily engaged in teaching academic subjects)

• Gambling businesses

• Businesses involved in speculation

• Lending and investment businesses (with the exception of pawn shops that deal primarily with the sale of merchandise)

• Pyramid sales distribution plans

Small Business Investment Companies (SBICs)

An alternative to traditional venture capital is financing from a Small Business Investment Company. SBICs are privately owned and managed venture capital firms licensed and regulated by the SBA that provide equity capital and long-term loans (up to 20 years) to small independent businesses. Specialized Small Business Investment Companies (SSBICs) target their funds to socially and economically disadvantaged owners of small businesses.

If you've been turned down for a bank loan due to insufficient assets or present income, or if your capital needs are too small to be attractive to large private venture capital firms, you should investigate the possibility of getting SBIC financing. SBICs will provide financing from $250,000 to $4 million. To be eligible for SBIC financing, you must meet the SBA's definition of "small business." For most industries, this translates as having a net worth of $18 million or less and average after-tax earnings of less than $6 million for the preceding two years.

The advantages to this type of financing are that SBIC management and directors must demonstrate a level of business expertise and professional talent before the firm is granted its license. This expertise can complement your own skills and you can turn to the experts for advice. Further, SBICs are prohibited from taking control of companies in which they invest, so you know you're not giving up the helm in return for capital.

There are over 200 SBICs and nearly 100 SSBICs nationwide. Most of them are listed in a directory published by the National Association of Small Business Investment Companies (NASBIC), the SBIC national trade association. To decide which SBIC you should contact, consider

the amount of financing you require, whether you need an equity investment or a loan, and where the SBIC is located, since many SBICs prefer to invest in companies nearby. In addition, most SBICs specialize in
particular industries, so pick one that likes to invest in yours. You can
find all this information in the directory, which you can get by contacting:

National Association of Small Business Investment Companies
666 11th St. NW, Suite 750
Washington, DC 20001
(202) 628-5055
Web site: http://www.nasbic.org

If you decide that SBIC funding is the right path for you, you'll be in
good company. Some of the largest and most well-known companies in
the country today—Federal Express, America Online, Intel, Cray
Research, and Apple Computer, for example—received SBIC backing.

MINORITY BUSINESS DEVELOPMENT AGENCY

The MBDA is a Commerce Department arm with approximately 100 centers throughout the country, concentrated in areas with large minority populations.
Contact your center to get your company listed in a database that is used by government agencies to identify minority-owned firms that can supply them with goods and services.
Centers can also counsel minority businesspeople on business planning, marketing, finance and more.

U.S. Department of Commerce,
Minority Business Development Agency
14th and Constitution Ave. N.W., Room 5073
Washington, DC 20230
(202) 482-1926

Xerox to build a portable plain paper copier that ran on batteries. However, Xerox was willing to back him in a separate company that eventually produced the copier.

Venture Capital

Venture capitalists specialize in investing sizable amounts of money, usually between $250,000 and $3 million, in new companies. In exchange, the VCs, as they're known, will take an ownership share and, sometimes, a management position. In a few years, they hope to sell out through an initial public offering (a stock offering on Wall Street) or other means and generate an annual return of 30 percent or more on their money.

Many highly successful companies, including Jobs' and Wozniak's fledgling Apple, got their first major backing from a VC. But fewer than 1 percent of start-ups get any venture capital financing. Why? Their steep return on investment requirements means your company must have very strong prospects for growth and profitability. If you can meet them and you can craft a convincing business plan, the VC tap may be open. Think long and hard before you go the venture capitalist route because there will be a lot of hoops to jump through in order to convince a VC that you are worthy of her investment. Don't bother trying if you aren't prepared to wait anywhere from six months to a year or more before you see one red cent.

Initial Public Offering of Stock (IPO)

An IPO represents the pot of gold at the end of the rainbow for many small business people and their financial backers. It allows you to sell shares in your corporation (IPOs are for corporations only) to the general public through such stock markets as the New York Stock Exchange and Nasdaq. It is probably the least expensive way to raise very large amounts of money. You don't have to sell your whole company, just whatever percent of it you can do without or your financing needs require.

Public offerings are generally only for businesses that have been in operation for some time, although you don't necessarily need profits or even sales to go public. A few start-ups, like Netscape Communications founded by Internet software pioneer Marc Andreessen, raised many millions of dollars largely on untapped potential.

The main IPO objection is that it involves complying with reams of rules, filing many documents with securities regulators, and, last but not least, paying major accounting and legal fees. Even a small IPO is likely to cost you $100,000 or more, just to obtain the right to make the offering. Getting your balance sheet, income statements, and accounting practices in shape may take a year or more. And, once you've gone public, everyone from shareholders to regulators will eye every move you make. Your plans may take a backseat to keeping up quarterly earnings growth, hiking the stock price, and the like. An IPO is a pot of gold with a price.

GET PAID IN ADVANCE

One way to avoid financing your business is to get paid in advance. It's common practice in many industries and professions to get part of the payment for a product or service at the time it is ordered. Advance payment helps you greatly by making it possible to hire necessary employees, obtain equipment and facilities, and keep current with your own suppliers without having to borrow money. Here are some professionals who customarily receive part or all of their money up front:

• Attorneys

• Book authors

• Custom manufacturers

• Consultants

• Furniture retailers

• Home builders

• Pet trainers

• Public relations consultants

How Does SBA LowDoc Work?

The Low Documentation (LowDoc) Loan Program is SBA's most popular loan. Under LowDoc, the SBA guarantees up to 90 percent of a $100,000 or less loan made by a commercial lender. Advantages include:

• It's a streamlined application process—the application form for loans under $50,000 is only one page. (For larger loans up to $100,000 the applicant needs to supply the last three years' income tax returns, personal financial statements from other guarantors and business co-owners, and cash flow projections.)

• Full collateral is not required. Instead, LowDoc takes into account the applicant's credit history and character.

• Close to 90 percent of applicants obtain financing.

• The loan approval process usually takes less than a week.

• Interest rates are tied to the prime rate and may be fixed or variable but cannot exceed SBA maximums.

In addition to meeting general requirements for SBA loans, LowDoc further requires that the average annual sales of your business do not exceed $5 million and that you employ less than 100 people, including affiliates.

For more information, contact the Small Business Administration at (800) 827-5722.

Small Company Offering Registration

A SCOR is a way, simpler than an initial public offering, for small companies to raise equity capital by selling stock to the public. The big difference is that you have only to file a single, relatively straightforward form to register your shares for sale in all but, at last count, four states. That cuts the cost for a stock offering considerably compared to a full-fledged IPO.

SCORs do have limits, however. You can raise no more than $1 million from a SCOR, while there is no ceiling on the amount you can raise from an IPO. And most SCOR issuers' stocks are not listed on the major exchanges, such as the New York Stock Exchange or Nasdaq. That limits the number of people who might buy your shares.

Corporate Bonds

A bond is basically an IOU that you sell someone, promising to repay them with interest at a later date. You set the amount, term, and rate at whatever you think investors will pay. You don't have to apply for a loan; you set the terms and offer them to lenders. (As with IPOs, however, there are quite a few regulations regarding sales of bonds to the public.)

Bonds' low costs compared to most other forms of borrowing make them the preferred method of debt financing for major companies. They often carry long terms—10 to 30 years or even longer—so they're good for financing long-lived assets such as machinery and facilities. The problem? It's hard for start-ups to satisfy the concerns of wary bond investors. You may have to wait until you're established to raise cash this way.

Bond issues are normally arranged by Wall Street investment firms. If you're considering seeking

WHAT IF YOU GET TURNED DOWN?

If you've exhausted all of your financing options and nobody has cut you a check, either:

• Your idea isn't a good one and you might want to head back to the drawing board.

or

• You aren't marketing your idea well enough and you need to revisit your business plan.

this type of long-term financing, ask your stockbroker or accountant for a referral to an investment firm's corporate finance department.

Where to Learn More

- *New Venture Mechanics* by Karl H. Vesper, published by Prentice Hall, 1992. This 380-page book by a well-regarded college teacher of entrepreneurialism is encyclopedic in scope and packed with case studies.

- *Guts & Borrowed Money: Straight Talk for Starting and Growing Your Small Business* by Tom S. Gillis, published by National Book Network, 1997. This 474-page manual for starting a business includes an alphabetical guide to 265 critical topics from raising money to finding vendors.

- *Self-Defense Finance for Small Business* by Wilbur Yegge, published by John Wiley & Sons, 1995. Yegge's advice is especially valuable when he tells you how to write business plans and financial statements, and create the other documents essential to dealing with banks and investors.

- *Borrowing to Build Your Business* by George M. Dawson, published by Dearborn Financial Publishing, Inc., 1997. Dawson gives the reader inside information on securing a loan.

- *America's Business Funding Directory,* at http://www.finance.com/search.htm. This Web site aims to hook up businesses that need funding, with investors. Search its listings of potential backers by looking for the type of financing you're after.

GETTING *your front* doors **OPEN**

CHAPTER EIGHT

The day you actually open the doors of your business calls for a **party.** *You'll deserve one— that day is preceded by quite a bit of planning, deciding, and acting.*

Considerations that need to be worked out before opening include selecting a site, finding employees, getting suppliers, obtaining distribution, setting prices, preparing for taxes, procuring accounting and legal advice, and lining up insurance coverage. A daunting list? To be sure. But millions before you have done it. Taking it a step at a time, you can get your doors open in good shape to succeed.

If you're opening a fast-food restaurant, selecting a location is among the most crucial decisions you face. A block too far off the highway, or a block too near a lower-priced competitor, and you may seal your fate before you flip your first burger. Same goes for most retail stores and services such as dry cleaners.

Location is also an important variable for other businesses. If you're going to manufacture heavy machinery you will want to be close to a rail or other transportation artery to cut down on the costs of shipping your product. If you're an art gallery owner, you will likely cluster close to other galleries to benefit from the concentration of customers.

TRY IT HIS WAY

When you're scouting locations, you may find surprising opportunities in unlikely places. Houston, in the midst of its oil recession in the early 1990s, didn't look too appealing to most new businesses. But Charlie Wilson of SeaRail International, a salvage company, was able to take advantage of low-priced warehouse space, a supply of unemployed labor, the existing transportation infrastructure, and a supportive community eager to attract commerce. When you're looking for office space, sometimes the best deals can be made in depressed areas or in converted warehouses.

Add it up and, in most businesses, location may not be the only factor determining your success, but it's often one of a handful that does. There is a host of standard considerations when choosing a site for your business, including traffic patterns, rental rates, environmental restrictions, zoning, and quality of life.

The first question to ask is: Who are my customers? Put together an ideal customer profile, describing the age, gender, income, interests, and other key traits of someone most likely to buy from you.

Next: Where are my customers? Finding out where they are is a matter of checking over U.S. Census Bureau data, yellow pages phone books, corporate directories, and the like. If you plan to open a children's indoor play facility, your ideal location will be close to a heavy concentration of families with young children and enough disposable income to afford you.

Close may not be good enough if traffic patterns steer your prospects away. Your location should have as many as possible of your ideal customers passing near it daily. Frequently, that's going to mean a location near a popular entrance of a shopping mall, a busy street or corner, or a space by a

heavily used freeway exit. You can get traffic analyses from your city economic development office or chamber of commerce.

Check also the mode of transportation passersby use. Lots of foot traffic isn't ideal if you're selling mufflers, brake jobs, and front-end alignments. Access is also important: If you will operate a small specialty lumber wholesaler, you'll need a place where trucks can easily drive in, back up, and load.

Competition is always a concern, not always for the same reasons. While a gourmet bagel shop might not want to be across the street from a similar store, a used-car dealer is likely to love a site along the local Motor Mile. Think about whether you'll benefit more from being the only game in town, or if the presence of similar businesses will attract more customers.

Zoning is an issue for all businesses. Zoning authorities decide what kind of business is commercial, what kind is industrial, and where each kind can locate. Zoning may also control your parking, signage, traffic, and environmental emissions. Many cities take an interest in regulating even home-based businesses that put up out-of-place signs, or boost the number of automobiles driving or parking in residential areas. Check zoning regulations at your city or county planning office. It's not a difficult thing to do, but it's one of those things that can sabotage you in a moment if you're not aware of the laws in your area.

Rent is crucial to start-ups. But don't automatically take the cheapest place you can find. A better location may produce more sales or lower costs of operation, resulting in higher profits than a cheaper spot would. And don't forget to factor in costs such as the landlord's willingness to share expenses for improving the space. One store-owner failed in a low-rent place, then succeeded with his second business located just 40 feet closer to the high-traffic area. Of course, if you're starting your business out of your home, you needn't worry about rent. You will, however, need to be aware of the IRS requirements for setting up your office.

Notice that not all considerations are of equal importance for all businesses. Zoning issues that could dent the prospects of an auto paint-and-body shop might be irrelevant to someone opening an acting agency. When you select where you are going to operate, you will want to look at your business's unique needs.

Locationless Businesses

Location is not crucial to all businesses. If you publish an investment newsletter, you can probably do it as well from Vail, Colorado, as from Wall Street (and many do). As a general rule, businesses that move information rather than physical goods are not particularly location sensitive. Here are some business examples with a low location sensitivity:

- Artists and graphic designers

- Freelance writers and editors

- Internet marketers

- Mail order marketers

- Management consultants

- Newsletter publishers

- Retailers of rare or hard-to-find products

- Telemarketers

- Utility bill auditors

Remember that every business has to be somewhere and, even if it's not crucial, location does make a difference. If you're a motivational speaker whose only office is at home, you might theoretically be able to ply your trade from a beach in Hawaii. But if you spend 200 days a year on the road, as many speakers do, your quality of life may actually be higher if you live and work near a major airport.

Finding Employees

Whether you're planning to work with a single partner or build a large staff, your business's most valuable assets will be its people. And your ability to locate and hire

talented and dedicated people will be a significant determinant of your success. Many a successful businessperson has credited his success to no more than an ability to surround himself with talented individuals. Be mindful, however, because adding people to the mix changes everything from the amount of your overhead to the interpersonal chemistry in your office. Here's a three-step plan for smart staffing.

Step One: Know Your Needs

Study carefully the requirements of every job you're trying to fill. Then write them down in job descriptions. Here's a sample job description for a speechwriter's research assistant.

Title: Research Assistant

Reports To: Director of Research

Duties: Locate current articles on selected topics, make copies, classify and file them by topic, retrieve them when needed.

Skills Required: Computer literacy, online database search knowledge, library research skills, good organizational ability.

Permits and Licenses Needed: Library card, driver's license (for visiting library).

Hours: Approximately 15 to 20 per week. Flexible.

TRY IT HER WAY

One challenge home-based businessowners face is where to hold meetings. If you have a section of your house set up as a real office, you have no problem. But many home-basers run operations from living rooms, kitchens, and even bedrooms—fine for phoning and working alone, but inappropriate when you're meeting face-to-face. Mary Lou Bessette, head of Bessette & Co., a home-based consulting firm in Phoenix, looked to the Arizona State Chamber of Commerce for the solution—she uses its office for her client meetings.

Once you've written descriptions for the first several positions you'll need to fill, boil them down into a staffing strategy. This will describe all the people you plan to hire in the first year, and will provide you with a road map to collecting valuable people.

Step Two: Look Before You Leap

Your first impulse may be to place a classified ad in the paper or hang a "help wanted" sign in the window. These can be effective hiring tools, but not for all ventures. If you need highly skilled workers, a sign in the window is likely to bring in far more undesirable candidates than desirable ones. Here are likely places to look before you leap with a hiring notice:

- *Classified ads.* You can reach thousands of people who self-select (by looking under the right classification in the paper) with a single inexpensive classified ad. To see if your local paper is a good place to hire the person you need, check for ads like the one you're placing. If your pet store needs a dog groomer and there's a whole category for them, you're in luck. More is better here. Very few ads like yours mean few qualified candidates will look here.

- *Help wanted signs.* Placing signs in your window is a great way to attract local help—and there's no cheaper way to advertise. But if you need special abilities, you'll have to look at a more selective audience. Use help wanted signs to hire for fast-food restaurants, counter help in dry cleaners and other retail service firms, and the like.

- *Family and friends.* Hiring people you know can be a great way to find dedicated help, but it can also be a source of sticky situations. If you have a friend who is eager to work and whose skills match your needs, then go for it. But don't hire friends and family just because you know them, especially if they are likely to take advantage of the fact that they "know" the owner.

- *Employment agencies.* There are many types of agencies. Government agencies are low-cost but slow. Private agencies cost more but may not have as many applicants as publicly supported ones. Trade unions can operate as specialty agencies for skilled craftspeople. If you're pulling wire in a large city, union electricians may be your only option. And don't forget career counselors at local colleges. They may direct you to a job posting bulletin board, or have just the right recently minted graduate at hand.

- *Temporary agencies.* If you're opening a pool cleaning service or a Christmas decoration store, you'll need seasonal workers. If your business consists of big projects with slow spells in between, like grant proposal writing or market research consulting, you're likely to need temporary workers to help you through busy times. In either case, a temp agency may be for you. These agencies are the actual employers of the people they send to you. The agency interviews and hires them, pays their wages, collects their taxes, and provides them with benefits. You only pay the temp agency. When you no longer need the employees, you simply send them back to the agency without any severance hassles. The drawback is, you pay a premium so the temp agency can make a profit. Even if your business isn't particularly seasonal or uneven, you may want to look at a temp agency in the beginning. It can save you most of the paperwork and effort involved in hiring permanent employees in the early days, when you may need to focus on other things. Hiring temporary employees is also the best way to try people out. If you like someone the temp agency sends you, consider hiring them on as full time.

- *Executive search firms.* Also known as headhunters, executive search firms charge you a fee to find just the right executive for you. Their fee usually equals a percentage of the employee's first year salary. Costs can easily reach many thousands of dollars, especially for a skilled technical or management person. The plus side is, headhunters do most of the work of screening and may provide high quality people with very specific skills. If you're a computer software developer in need of immediate programming expertise for an esoteric problem, you may find a headhunter specializing in high tech with a Rolodex full of perfect candidates. In general, however, only call on headhunters if nothing else works.

Step Three: Interview Carefully and Follow Up

Always use written applications to gather basic information about applicants. Then, select the most promising and have them come in for a talk. Craft questions that will find candidates that fit your job descriptions. Ask them and note the answers. Then

reflect on them again in private. Now is also the time to check references for past employment. You may not get much, and what you do may be of questionable value—few employers emphasize giving good references to ex-employees—but do it. As hard as hiring is, it's easier than firing an employee who doesn't work out.

Employment Legal Issues

Discrimination in employment is a serious issue for employers. When you're interviewing, you may be in legal hot water if you ask questions about an applicant's age, race, religion, place of birth, marital status, native language, or even military service.

It's okay to ask if an applicant is over 18. You may also ask your applicant if he or she can provide proof of age if hired. While you can't ask about citizenship status, you can ask if a worker can, if hired, prove she has the right to work in the United States. And, while you can't ask about physical handicaps, it's okay to ask if an applicant has a condition that would prevent her from doing the job.

Getting Suppliers

Every business has suppliers. Even if you're planning a home-based business auditing medical bills, you'll need telephone service, stationery, a desk, chair, and filing cabinet. In addition, it's hard to think of a business that doesn't require an answering machine, computer, fax machine, and their necessary supplies. For all of these needs, cost and quality are important—and depend on the suppliers you select.

For retailers, restaurants, or manufacturers, suppliers are even more critical. Having reliable, low-cost, high-quality sources for the goods and materials you buy for resale can make a big contribution toward helping an otherwise marginal business prosper. This isn't just about getting a contract as exclusive distributor of some hard-to-find item. An antiques dealer with a gift for gabbing with country folk may have a big edge over other dealers when it comes to snapping up local heirlooms for her shop.

Smart businesspeople take advantage of their suppliers in other ways too. Ellen Oprandy spent six months preparing to open her pet supply store. She spent most of

that time cultivating good suppliers who would deliver inventory to her on time and at a good price. After a doing lot of research and spending some time interviewing other pet shop owners in the area, Ellen found a great dog food supplier who agreed to split the cost of her newspaper advertising if she included his logo in her ads. (That's called co-op advertising and a lot of suppliers will do it if you ask for it.) They also gave her 90-day credit terms on her initial orders and provided her with a big bag of dog bones to give away to her best customers. A cat grooming supply distributor gave her advertising signage for her front window, some in-store display units, and a newsletter on grooming techniques she could use as a mailer to promote her store. The suppliers have a big stake in Ellen's success. If the store succeeds, then Ellen will keep buying from them.

Good suppliers will go a long way towards helping their retailers market their businesses. If you're buying a lot of something, you can get discounts, customer referrals and technical help, marketing materials such as camera-ready artwork, co-op advertising, and more from your suppliers.

A computer consultant who specializes in setting up companies with a specific contact management software package can expect sales leads, telephone support for customers, and probably free training from the software's maker.

The flip side of suppliers is that choosing the wrong one can be a liability. Developing a dependence on a supplier who is unreliable or dishonest, or one who provides low-quality merchandise, could severely handicap you.

Here's a three-step process to making the most of suppliers:

1. *Ask for referrals.* Question associates in the same business to learn from whom they buy and what their experience has been. Look for suppliers who have what you need, who deliver it as ordered, on time, and who offer generous terms. Expand your list by checking directories such as the yellow pages, your city's manufacturer directories, and your local library's copy of the *Thomas Register of Manufacturers.* Call or write to get catalogs, price lists, available terms, and other information.

2. *Sell yourself.* Buying as a business isn't the same as being a consumer. You're not king until you prove you're a good customer. Getting good treatment from suppliers requires convincing them you will pay bills in full and on time, you'll order in sufficient quantity to make it worth their while, and you won't require excessive attention. The effort will pay off in better terms and better treatment. Without it, you're likely to find yourself dealing with uninterested salespeople, slow service, and COD required on every order. Unfortunately, many suppliers have been burned selling to poorly planned start-ups that never become profitable customers.

3. *Look beyond price.* Once you've established that you're a good business to sell to, you can start taking advantage of lots of goodies that ordinary consumers don't get. A bar owner may be able to get 60- or 90-day extended credit terms or, on the flip side, discounts of 1 or 2 percent for paying the liquor wholesaler's delivery driver in cash. The same bar owner may be able to better match his cash inflow to cash outflow by requesting more frequent, smaller deliveries rather than having to pay for a month's worth of supplies at a time. Suppliers may even pay you, in the form of cooperative advertising, incentive prizes, or other inducements.

Suppliers can be a businessowner's headache or helper. Careful selection of the right ones in the beginning can go a long way toward resolving the issue.

Obtaining Distribution

Distribution is the process of getting goods from the factory to the user. If you're a small publisher, your product is a book. You edit, print, and bind it. You then ship it to a book distributor or wholesaler. Next, it is transported to a bookstore. Finally, a reader purchases it and takes it home.

These four entities—manufacturer, wholesaler/distributor, retailer, and end user—make up a traditional distribution channel. (Sometimes an agent or broker substitutes for a wholesaler.) They can be combined in a variety of ways, and there are lots of alternative modes of distribution. They include mail order, telemarketing, multilevel marketing, vending machines, door-to-door sales, and, lately, marketing through the

A Sobering Thought

 You will end up getting involved in the lives of the people who work for you, whether you want to or not—and you'll find you may be able to make a difference. Of course, making sure your employees steer clear of substance abuse makes sense from a business standpoint—a drug-free business is one with low employee turnover and high productivity. Here are some government resources that can help:

• Drug Free Workplace Helpline, (800) 843-4971
For information on Employee Assistance Programs (EAPs), workplace-based alcohol and substance abuse programs

• National Institute for Drug Abuse Hotline, (800) 662-4357
For information on preventing substance abuse in the workplace

• National Clearinghouse for Alcohol and Drug Information, (800) 729-6686
For pamphlets and other resources on substance abuse

U.S. DEPARTMENT OF LABOR

To get up to speed on the labor laws and how they'll affect your business, you can request publications from:

U.S. Department of Labor
Employment Standards
Administration
200 Constitution Ave. NW
Washington, DC 20210
(202) 219-8743

Internet. How you get your goods to market is a matter to decide before you open your doors. Here's how the options stack up:

Direct distribution is simplest. You make something and sell it straight to the end user. A custom home builder operates this way, building spec homes on lots he purchases and marketing them himself directly to home buyers.

The advantage of direct distribution is that it cuts out the middleman. Each time a product goes through a link in the chain of distribution, the company representing that link adds something to the price. A book wholesaler may mark up the latest bestseller by 50 to 100 percent of his cost before selling it to a bookstore, which tacks on a similar markup before selling it to someone heading for a beach vacation. If the book's publisher could sell direct to that beach reader, he could get two to four times as much per book.

The problem with direct distribution is that it's expensive and difficult, especially for small companies, to have the geographic reach and marketing resources to sell direct to large markets. How is our small publisher going to sell you the book without having a store in your town? One answer is by direct marketing through the mail, the telephone, or the Internet. These direct distribution channels are frequently very appropriate for small companies because of their low cost and high margins. It can be difficult to achieve significant volume in a direct distribution scheme, but cutting out the middlemen can make up for it.

The next simplest distribution involves selling to retailers, who sell to end users. This solves the retail-distribution problem for manufacturers. Now instead of our small publisher selling to millions of potential consumers, he has only to sell to a few thousand bookstores. This reduces his need to do extensive advertising and hire a large force of people to take orders for one book at a time.

Adding wholesalers and distributors to the distribution channel lets a product maker sell to many more retailers. A wholesaler is a middleman who provides bulk goods and services to retailers (or sometimes even to end consumers), while distributors usually have their own sales forces who are experienced at selling to local or special markets that may lie outside the expertise of a manufacturer. Wholesalers and distributors may add value by repackaging or even relabeling products to fit specific market needs. Using wholesalers also opens up a whole new market: Large organizational buyers and bargain-hunting consumers who buy from wholesale or warehouse-type sources.

Agents and brokers can fill roles similar to wholesalers and distributors, selling your products to retailers, distributors, and end users. But, while wholesalers actually pay for and take delivery of your goods before reselling them to retailers or end users, agents only line up orders for you to fill. They typically add little or no value compared to distributors or wholesalers. And, they are usually paid by commission, similarly to salespeople. The benefit of agents is that there are more of them and they are easier to sign up than full-fledged wholesalers. If you're planning to sell overseas, you'll find agents and brokers are important distribution channels.

Which channel is right for you? To start with, the channel that most people in your industry use ought to be a good fit. However, there's often an advantage to breaking the mold. Wal-Mart's practice of going direct to manufacturers, bypassing distributors, is part of the strategy that made it the country's biggest retailer. Dell Computer, which sells direct to consumers and businesses, has been so successful that more traditional competitors are beginning to try to copy its distribution style.

Some of the alternative distribution channels are attractive to start-up businesses. They tend to be low-cost, high-margin channels without existing dominant competitors. Although volumes may not be as high as in traditional distribution channels, they deserve a look.

FREE TAX INFORMATION

The IRS has all kinds of free information on tax requirements for small businesses. Contact them at:

U.S. Department of Treasury,
Internal Revenue Service (IRS)
1111 Constitution Ave. NW
Washington, DC 20224
(800) 829-1040
(202) 622-5000

Setting Prices

Everything has its price—what's yours going to be? Setting prices is one of the things you'll have to do before opening your doors. To do so, you should understand the methods of setting prices and the possible effects of pricing too low or too high.

Pricing Strategies

Most entrepreneurs base pricing on their cost, plus what they consider a fair profit. If you figure it will cost you $8 to give a haircut in your new salon, and you need to show a $6 profit per cut, your price would be $14. There's nothing wrong with this cost-plus pricing. It's simple and at least guarantees you'll cover costs and show a profit on any sales you make. But there are other legitimate objectives for a pricing plan.

You may want to set prices low to build volume or to quickly grab market share. Another objective of low prices may be to discourage competition or to drive rivals out of the market. If you're beginning a landscaping service and notice your main future rival is using worn-out equipment and low-quality labor, you may up the pressure on him in hopes of having the market to yourself.

You may set prices high, on the other hand, to discourage price slashing. High prices also can help establish your company as a premium provider. Remember Gary, the hair salon owner featured in chapter three? He set his prices high in order to help position his salon as the most upscale place in town. A low pricing strategy would have worked counter to his positioning statement. His clients interpreted his higher prices to mean higher quality.

High prices may also be necessary to recover your development costs for a new product. If you are

SUPPLY-SIDE ECONOMICS

Your future suppliers can be terrific sources for information about the market. They'll be eager to help because you are a potential customer and by sharing their knowledge of the market with you they are actually strengthening their own businesses. They may even be willing to share the results of market research and will certainly be able to furnish you with all sorts of tips about the people you'll be dealing with.

temporarily the only supplier for a cutting edge product or service, you may keep prices high simply to maximize your own profits before competition sets in.

And don't forget that there is more to pricing than slapping on labels bearing dollar amounts. Will you have regular sales? Or everyday low prices? Will your prices include all necessary accessories, service, and support? Or will you be a bare-bones dealer, charging extra for everything but the basic item? If you are starting a nanny referral service, will you let clients deduct the $50 application from the $300 placement fee if they hire a nanny from you? These are more than quiz questions. They're basic tools in how you price what you sell.

PRICING EQUATION

Use this equation when you're determining your prices:

cost + operating expenses + desired profit = price

Be careful about reducing prices in hopes of making it up on volume. Always do the math before changing your prices and make sure you're looking at the bottom line. Here's an example. Let's say you have a product that sells for $1.00 and it costs you 75 cents to make. That means you make a profit of 25 cents a unit. If you drop your price 10 percent, you make 15 cents a unit. That means you've got to sell nearly twice as many to make the same amount of money. If you raise your price 10 cents, on the other hand, your profit is 35 cents. That means that sales could drop a whole bunch —you sell three instead of four—and you still come out way ahead.

Taxes

Small business ownership won't let you escape taxes, but it does have advantages as well as some disadvantages. There is a host of deductions you can take and tax incentives you should be aware of once you start your business.

If you are a real estate agent working from a home office, for example, you may now be able to deduct many costs, including a portion of your mortgage and utilities, as business expenses. On the downside, you'll have to file additional forms, including a Schedule C and possibly other forms for partnerships and corporations. And if you

Business Incubators

Operated by state and local governments, colleges and universities, and private companies, business incubators are alternatives to home offices or costly long-term leases. They provide start-ups with affordable space (usually at below-market rates) and shared support services like phone answering, bookkeeping, word processing, and administrative assistance, and access to copiers, fax machines, and computers.

In addition, business incubators offer fledgling entrepreneurs the chance to take advantage of technical support, training programs, and networking opportunities. Like a new mother who joins a parenting group, you gain a tremendous amount of knowledge from being around other small businesses, seeing the challenges they face, and how they solve them. But taking this one step further, all these contacts may translate into new suppliers or even customers.

Business incubators can also help with financing by sharing tips on how to get bank loans or take advantage of government funds.

To get a listing of the incubators in your area:

National Business Incubation Association
20 East Circle Dr., Suite 190
Athens, OH 45701
(614) 593-4331
Web site: http://www.NBIA.org
e-mail: smckinnon@NBIA.org

have employees your tax complications multiply rapidly. Your best bet is to get some professional advice. Contact the SBA for some basic information, but get a professional accountant to set you up and get you going. Mistakes in the tax area can cost you big time in the long run. Make sure you do it right the first time.

Figuring and paying estimated taxes is one of the biggest differences between working for yourself and working for someone else. As an employee, your employer is responsible for figuring your withholding, setting the money aside, and paying it to the proper taxing authorities. Now that you're self-employed, you do that yourself. Roughly every 90 days, you must estimate your earnings for that period, figure the taxes you owe on them, and send a check to the Internal Revenue Service.

It's a significant paperwork challenge and no small financial one. You may not have ever missed the amounts your employer was taking out of your check. But be prepared for a shock the first time you write out a quarterly estimate check.

Unfortunately, too many businesses are indeed shocked by taxes. It is critical that you figure and set aside accurate amounts for income, Social Security, Medicare, and sales taxes, for yourself as well as any employees. Federal, state, and local taxing authorities can and will lock the doors of your business, auction off the contents, and even pursue you for criminal prosecution if you flout the tax laws, whether through ignorance or inattention.

While taxes are hardly becoming less complicated, it is becoming easier to figure and file your estimated taxes and final returns. That's because of the development of powerful and inexpensive tax-filing software that runs on any personal computer. Programs such as TurboTax Deluxe from Intuit or Kiplinger TaxCut by Block Financial are adequate for filing many small business returns, are fairly simple to use, and cost a fraction of what you would pay a Certified Public Accountant (CPA). Again, your accounting professional can set you up for estimated tax payments.

Most states have sales taxes (sometimes called use taxes) that are charged on all final sales to consumers. Sales taxes are not usually charged on business-to-business sales such as between manufacturers and wholesalers. Sales taxes may also be levied by transportation authorities and other public entities.

Try It Their Way

The Circuit Board is an informal advisory board of five entrepreneurs in the Boston area, all of whom are heads of companies that have less than 20 employees.

Four of them are from corporate backgrounds, and when they became CEOs of their own companies, they found they missed the networking benefits of being part of a large firm—the access to peers and free expert advice that you get by working for a big organization. So David Corbett, Robert Schmidt, George Bixby, Don Aikman, and Dale Lattanzio visit each other's companies, watch each other's operations, meet with each other's managers and employees, and get together every two months to discuss one of the businesses.

Each brings a particular brand of expertise: Corbett, who runs an executive outplacement firm, specializes in marketing; Schmidt, the drapery manufacturer, is the operations guru; Bixby is a manufacturer's rep who knows about international suppliers; Aikman, the putty manufacturer, contributes a knowledge of working with distributors; and Lattanzio, a print distributor, shows fellow Circuit Boarders how to increase sales.

By observing and critiquing each other's businesses, members of the Circuit Board have minimized errors and learned a tremendous amount from sharing their ideas.

Sales taxes are commonly based on a percentage of the value of the item or service sold. They are often not charged on various products, such as basic foodstuffs. Some services are also exempt.

It is generally the responsibility of the retailer to collect and remit sales taxes to the proper authorities at stated intervals. Specific requirements vary widely according to locality. Contact your state collection or reporting office for details and forms. Look in the phone book's government pages for your state under sales tax, taxes, treasurer, comptroller, or a similar heading.

Accounting and Bookkeeping Help

If you are a one-person business and have the time and inclination to keep the books and prepare tax returns, you probably don't need an accountant or bookkeeper. But when you begin to add employees, apply for business loans, seek investors, set up retirement plans, or handle complex financial issues, you are likely to need professional help.

A personal referral is the best way to find an accountant or bookkeeper. You're going to be sharing intimate financial details with this individual. Get someone you trust. But make sure that whomever you hire knows your field. Accounting for a manufacturing company is very different from accounting for a service firm. Make sure your accountant is up-to-date with all of the latest rules and regulations affecting your industry.

Ask friends, relatives, and associates whom they use. Set up appointments to talk with the candidates. Look for someone who communicates well. Discuss your goals and problems. Discuss the accountant's experience, training, and style. Find out early on what the fee is likely to be. Get fee schedules nailed down in writing with an engagement letter before your final selection.

You can probably start with a part-time bookkeeper, perhaps one or two days a month. Someone who also prepares tax returns would be extra useful. If you require audited financials for any reason, such as applying for a loan, you can get a Certified Public Accountant to look over your books on a one-time basis.

Later on, as your financial complexities mount, you may want to hire a full-time book-keeper, and have a CPA regularly review the books and handle special projects such as tax filings. Avoid the so-called Big Six accounting firms in favor of a small local accounting firm or individual. You don't need all of the high-octane services one of the Big Six can supply, nor do you need to pay the fees that go along with them.

Accounting Software

In bookkeeping as in so many things, computers are making life easier. For a couple of hundred dollars or less, you can get software that runs on your office computer and easily handles double-entry accounting, inventory, and payroll. Most can also produce a wide variety of useful reports, such as receivables aging analyses. They also do payables, cut checks, and can handle most of the day-to-day functions you'll need to perform.

Programs such as Intuit's QuickBooks Pro or Peachtree's First Accounting are simple to use, inexpensive, and ample for many small businesses. If you are a solo self-employed, you can probably even use Quicken, the personal finance program from Intuit. As your business grows, you can move up to Peachtree's full-featured Complete Accounting or a similar program.

COMPLYING WITH THE EPA

EPA regulations are many and complex, but you can get help understanding them and learning how to make your business earth- and EPA-compatible using the resources of over 100 publications available from the agency. Contact the EPA at:

U.S. Environmental Protection Agency (EPA)
Small Business Ombudsman
401 M St. SW
Washington, DC 20460
(800) 368-5888
(202) 260-2090

Legal Advice

You may be in business for years without needing a lawyer. Many self-employed service providers, such as interior decorators, music teachers, and the like, never do. On the other hand, if you're even a small corporation, you'll need a lawyer on day one. And considering the likelihood of legal disputes over payment of bills, hiring and firing of employees,

and other matters, it's a good idea to have at least a casual relationship with a competent attorney you can call on in time of need.

You may need help with incorporating or drawing up a partnership agreement for your business. If you sign contracts for significant amounts, such as to purchase a building or expensive equipment, it's a good idea to have an attorney review them. If you manufacture toys, you may want to have a lawyer check out your liability disclaimer. And many other businesses have special needs that will benefit from the scrutiny of an appropriate attorney.

The best place to get a lawyer is through a friend's or business colleague's recommendation. As with an accountant, trust is important. Interview your attorney as carefully as you would an accountant or a new employee. Share your issues. Inspect his or her credentials and attitudes carefully. Don't shy away from asking about fees and terms.

If you have no recommendation or several to choose from, your local bar association can give you a referral. In general, avoid both large firms and one-attorney practices. The first is likely to be too expensive, the second too limited. A mid-sized firm will likely offer a combination of reasonable fees and broad expertise. Always ask for flat rate fees rather than hourly ones and get all estimates in writing. It's easy for legal fees to get out of hand fast. Make sure you know what you're spending up front.

TRY IT THEIR WAY

Chris Calande, Fred Ehnow, and Scott DeFreitas own Bit Jugglers, a successful software company in Mountain View, California. Because their product, UnderWare™, is a Macintosh-compatible screen saver, it was crucial for them to be located near Apple and at the center of the computer universe: Silicon Valley. This prime location also keeps them close to suppliers, creative talent, and the magazines that serve the industry. Before you choose a location, evaluate how important it is to be situated close to the center of your universe.

CASH FLOW TIPS

• Keep enough cash each month to pay the cash obligations of the next month.

• Too much cash may indicate excessive borrowing.

• Invest excess cash.

• Maintain monthly projections to keep track of cash flow.

Insurance

Insurance is one of the most commonly over-looked start-up needs. It's understandable; you are strapped for cash, you have to pay the premium now, and the possibility of needing insurance seems remote. Odds are, you won't ever collect a penny on many kinds of insurance coverage—otherwise the insurance companies wouldn't be in business long. But other types you will use (some types are required by law), and even if you never file a claim, having adequate paid-up insurance is a valuable aid to a good night's sleep.

You will be required, by the law or other entities, to carry some types of insurance. Lenders require insurance against loss on any property securing a loan. State and federal law requires you provide unemployment and workmen's compensation coverage for employees. Although it's not required by law, many companies provide employees with some kind of health coverage. And, if you have more than 100 employees and provide any of them with any kind of group insurance, federal law requires you to offer it to all workers.

Good business practice requires you to insure against loss by fire, theft, or other disaster of any asset that is critical to your business. That includes automobiles, computers, machinery, inventory, fixtures, and buildings.

You should also carry coverage against liabilities that may arise from any activities that you or your employees are likely to engage in. That may include coverage for vehicle damage, embezzlement, product liability, and the like. Depending on your business, you may be required to carry fidelity or performance bonds.

Key employee insurance is something many businesses carry to protect against the loss of a critical worker such as the founder or a technological wizard. Less common, because it's costly, is business-interruption insurance, designed to protect the business against losses resulting from some event that may interfere with the operation of the business.

You can get help from any business insurance agent. Again, you can use a personal referral to get started. But here the company behind the insurance is at least as important as the agent you're buying from. So don't feel bound by a friend's recommendation.

Any broker or agent will conduct an insurance survey for free. Discuss your view of your business's needs and your insurance concerns in addition to listening to the expert, who may never have seen a company like yours. After getting a few surveys from different brokers, compare both the costs and how these professionals assess your needs. Don't focus only on premiums. Higher deductibles and more exclusions can produce low premiums, but may be costly if you suffer a loss.

BOP Me

A businessowners policy (BOP) is a standard bundle of insurance for small stores, offices, and apartment buildings. A BOP protects a business's buildings and property against the usual risks. It may also provide business-interruption coverage, coverage against embezzlement or employee dishonesty, damage to outdoor signs, and various kinds of liability. Some BOPs have special features such as seasonal peak coverage for retailers who have extra heavy inventories during the holidays. Larger businesses, manufacturers, restaurants, contractors, motels, hotels, and others for which BOPs aren't available can use a standard commercial package policy (CPP). The CPP is more flexible, allowing you to pick and choose your coverage more selectively, but costs about a third more than a BOP.

Where to Learn More

- *How to Start and Run a Successful Consulting Business* by Gregory and Patricia Kishel, published by John Wiley & Sons, 1996. The Kishels are veteran small business management consultants with special expertise in working with the Small Business Administration. Their book is clear, concise, and complete.

- *Price Wars: A Strategy to Winning the Battle for the Customer* by Thomas J. Winninger, published by St. Thomas Press, 1995. You'll know all about how raising or lowering your prices will affect your customers and

profits after reading this 225-page, highly practical guide to the all-important art of pricing.

- *TurboTax/MacInTax,* by Intuit, (800) 446-8848. These are the best-sellers among personal tax preparation software, and are adequate for many self-employed people and small business owners, including partnerships. You can get supplements for filing most state tax returns for $24.95. Versions are available for Macintosh and Windows systems.

- *Free Business Stuff from the Internet* by Vince Emery and Patrick Vincent, published by Coriolis Group, 1996. This book shows users how to get hundreds of dollars worth of free business-related stuff from the Internet. You'll get the exact Internet location of great business freebies that will help users make money, build sales, boost productivity, and more.

- *CareerFile* at http://www.careerfile.com. You can post job openings and browse the database of candidates for free. Once you've found a candidate by browsing, it costs $6.95 to see a detailed résumé, including contact information.

- *Insurance Smart: How to Buy the Right Insurance at the Right Price* by Jeff O'Donnell, published by John Wiley & Sons, 1991. A no-holds-barred primer by a veteran agent on selecting all kinds of insurance.

IT'S REALLY *all about* sales and *promotion* ANYWAY!

CHAPTER NINE

You've planned out your strategy and opened your doors. Now it's time to get down to the business of **attracting** clients and customers, and making the most of them.

An athletic shoe company that buys 60 seconds during the Super Bowl is promoting its products. So is a New Orleans barker who buttonholes you on Bourbon Street to invite you into his bar for a half-price drink. Chances are, your start-up business won't employ either of these kinds of promotions. You're more likely to emphasize low-cost, high leverage promotional techniques, such as placing classified newspaper ads to attract customers to your used computer store, or putting up flyers to inform everyone in your neighborhood that you'll clean the window blinds in their homes.

One thing is certain: You will need some way to inform, persuade, and remind your customers and prospects that you have something they need. Promotion is how you do it.

A business with sales can survive almost anything. Sales bring cash, and cash can buy you a new factory, new employees, new products. But without sales, without the oomph you get from marketing, most new businesses fail.

There's way too much to cover in just a few pages. Instead, the purpose of this chapter is to highlight the basic techniques you'll be using and then point you to a book or two that can fill in the rest of the details. It may sound like a bit of work, but it's worth it!

If you're planning to start a business in which you already know all of your potential customers, this chapter won't be of much use. But if you need to find, contact, and convert strangers into customers, the ideas and references contained in this chapter are important for you to understand. In fact, marketing and promotion might be the most important things you do as a small business owner because if you don't have any customers, nothing much else matters.

TRY IT HER WAY

Use what professional writers have to say about you in your own advertising and promotion. Donna Salyers has a synthetic fur coat business. She found her positioning statement, "A Kinder, Gentler Fur Coat," when she saw it in a newspaper headline over an article about her business. She didn't come up with it herself, but she knew a good thing when she saw it.

The first thing to do when it comes to promoting your business is plan. Elaborate on the promotion part of the marketing plan you outlined in your business plan (or create one from scratch if you didn't write a business plan). In the process, you'll set goals, choose methods, identify your target market, select your niche, and figure out how much you'll spend.

Your Promotion Plan

You probably shouldn't even bother to promote your business without a plan. It's so easy to create

one, and extremely valuable once you've got it. A plan keeps you on track, ensuring that you deliver a consistent message to your target audience. Without a plan, you're liable to switch messages whenever the spirit moves you. Repeating a consistent message will make your promotion much more effective.

You can create a helpful promotion plan by answering just a few questions. Getting this far should take no more than a sheet or two of paper and a few minutes of time. Here are questions to ask, and some sample answers:

What (Exactly) Do You Hope to Achieve with Your Promotions?

The best way to describe your hopes for your promotion is in terms of the kind or number of customers you expect it to attract. But you can also express your goal in terms of building your name recognition or a particular image. For instance:

- Promotional activities for Springtime Landscape Design will lead to repeat customers and long-term contracts.

- The promotion for First Word Speakers Bureau will build a reputation for the bureau as the finest speaker's agency in the Tri-Valley Region.

- The start-up promotion plan for Glendale Animal Hospital will make its name known to a majority of pet owners within a five-mile radius.

TRY IT HIS WAY

Kevin Knight is a marketing consultant who was able to turn a single speaking engagement into more than a million dollars worth of sales. He followed up his marketing communications speech to a group of executives with a handout of some articles on the subject. A few days later, he sent thank-you letters to each member of the audience and offered to help with any problems they might have. His efforts were rewarded with a tremendous boost in business.

Who's Your Target Audience?

It's tempting to say that practically anybody could use your product or service. But who is most likely to use it? If you can't get specific, you don't have a target. You need to be able to visualize your best customer. That is your target audience. If you're opening a combination copy shop/postal center, you may define your most likely customers as nearby small business owners and home office workers. So, start with them.

- Springtime Landscape Design's target audience consists of apartment complexes, shopping centers, and office developments in the county.

- First Word Speakers Bureau's target audience consists of business book authors, employee trainers, and management consultants in the Tri-Valley area.

- Glendale Animal Hospital's target audience consists of exotic animal owners within a five-mile radius.

As a small business owner, you need to focus on relationship building and on selling to your best customers over and over. You're not McDonald's—you'll never have "billions and billions served." But if you're a freelance graphic artist with 25 steady clients, or a bicycle shop with 500 regular customers, that probably means your marketing is working.

What's Your Position in the Market?

Each and every type of promotion you do should convey your positioning statement to your target audience. Here are the positioning statements for our three example businesses:

- Springtime Landscape Design will be the commercial landscaping specialist for the county.

- First Word Speakers Bureau will be the number one supplier of business speakers in the Northeast.

- Glendale Animal Hospital will be the leading local treatment facility for exotic pets.

What Will Be Your Main Promotional Vehicles?

Your basic promotional tools are advertising (including mass media and direct marketing), personal selling, sales promotions (such as frequent buyer plans), and publicity. Every business relies more on some elements than others. Here are some examples:

- Springtime Landscape Design will make 20 personal sales calls weekly, offering 10 percent discounts for design and maintenance contracts of more than three months.

- First Word Speakers Bureau will personally guarantee in writing the satisfaction of any and every one of its clients, and ask for three referrals from every satisfied client that they can reprint on their business cards.

- Glendale Animal Hospital will place one-column-by-eight-inch advertisements next to the "About Pets" column in the *Glendale News* each Sunday for two weeks before its grand opening, and for six weeks thereafter. In addition, approximately 5,000 flyers will be distributed on car windshields at shopping malls, outside pet supply stores, and at competing animal hospitals within a five-mile radius.

TRY IT HIS WAY

Knowing that an envelope with a handwritten address will not be thrown in the garbage unread, freelance designer John Langdon addresses every piece of direct mail by hand.

This can get cumbersome if you're sending out a large mailing. However, there are direct mailing houses that will do this for you for a fee.

How Much Are You Going to Spend?

The amount you spend on promotion can vary greatly over time, but start out with a plan. Unfortunately, when money gets tight, too many businessowners begin by cutting the amount of money they spend on promotion. If you do that, however, you're just helping the well of business continue to dry up. Instead, focus on high impact, low-cost methods of promoting your business and stick with them.

- Springtime Landscape Design will devote two days per week to setting up and making personal sales calls.

- First Word Speakers Bureau will spend $100 on printing business cards with the written guarantee, and three hours per week asking current and former clients for referral business.

- Glendale Animal Hospital will allocate 12 percent of total projected revenues to promotional activities.

A plan is only a plan, and it must change to reflect reality. If yours is to be useful, update it at least annually or whenever business circumstances change radically. The abbreviated plans like the ones above naturally lack a lot of details. Read the next sections about advertising, personal selling, publicity, and sales promotions to figure out exactly what you can do.

Advertising

Advertising is probably the best-known and most widely used form of promotion. It includes everything from the commercials you watch during the Super Bowl to the paper beer company coaster you set your drink down on to cheer the big plays.

TRY IT HIS WAY

Siebel Systems is a San Mateo, California-based software company that has a unique interior design guaranteed to make clients feel important. Chairman and CEO Tom Siebel had the lobby and halls decorated with client logos, annual reports, and framed letters from customers, and named some of the rooms after clients. When these people pay a visit to Siebel, they know the company really cares about them.

When you call every manufacturer in the yellow pages to offer them your services as a provider of temporary employees, for instance, you're advertising through the medium of telemarketing.

Effective advertising calls for you to decide what you're going to say, how you're going to say it, where you're going to say it, and what you can spend on it. For small start-ups, the goal is to choose high impact, low-cost methods that reach highly targeted audiences.

You've already staked out your position in the marketplace. Now it's time to turn that position into an advertising theme. Your theme will be determined by your business's or product's strengths (and weaknesses) and your target market's traits. You may also consider your competition's strengths, weaknesses, and target markets. The goal is to come up with a message (or messages, if you have more than one product or market) that says what you want to say to the people you want to hear it.

TRY IT HER WAY

Everyone makes mistakes. The best way to deal with a boo-boo is to admit it, apologize, and make it up to your clients with a freebie of some sort. It worked for Marjorie Desgrosselier, a home-based information broker. Instead of giving up, she offered to do the job over at no charge. Not only was the customer happy with the new work, he came back again and again and ended up referring others.

Next, how do you want to convey your advertising message? Advertising includes print media such as magazines and newspapers and miscellaneous printed materials such as brochures, pamphlets, flyers, and matchbooks, and broadcast media like television and radio, as well as outdoor advertising (billboards).

Above all, the medium you pick must be seen or heard by your target audience. For a small business the cost-effectiveness of the medium is also crucial, with lower cost getting more emphasis. If you're providing toddler swimming lessons, three-by-five cards tacked to the bulletin boards of local daycare centers may be just as effective in reaching your intended audience of parents of young children as a network TV commercial. Since the card is cheaper, it gets the nod. Here are some low-cost advertising media many start-ups have used effectively:

- Ad specialties such as refrigerator magnets bearing your message

- Billboards

- Brochures

- Doorhangers

- Industry magazines and trade journals

- Local cable TV spots

- Local radio spots

- Matchbooks

- Newspaper classified ads

- Postcards

- Posters

- Printed flyers posted on bulletin boards

- Printed handbills slipped under windshield wipers

- Yellow pages ads

Few ads have no words in them. Most products are sold on the basis of verbal descriptions of the benefits they offer. The better your ad copy, the more effective (all things being equal) your advertising will be. This is true whether you're writing a blurb to go up for six months on a billboard beside a busy freeway interchange, or crafting a three-line classified ad that will run four Sundays in a newspaper and disappear.

TRY IT HER WAY

Roslyn Goldman has been a home-based art appraiser and consultant since 1985. To build a client base, she opted for a large-scale low-cost networking campaign. She became active in the arts community on a local and national level, she took on an art project at a nearby airport, she gave speeches about public art, and she worked on programs for art groups, museums, and libraries. These efforts paid off in ways far more valuable than cash. She established herself as an expert in her field, and made extensive contacts with key people who have continued to help her business grow through the years.

The most important words in any advertisement are in the headline. An ad headline should be short and carry an appeal near and dear to the hearts of your target audience. A good one will stop people in their tracks and get them to read the rest of the ad. A bad one will never get noticed at all. Here are some samples of arresting headlines:

- Need More Money?

- Want to Lose Weight?

- 1,000 Hot Sales Leads!

- PUPPIES PUPPIES PUPPIES

After your headline, the next most important parts are, in order, any special offers you are making, art or illustrations and captions, and, finally, the text or body copy.

You can hire a professional copywriter to word your ad for you. If you do, avoid agencies. Many of the best work alone and charge less than agencies. Seek someone experienced in your industry and your market. An automotive copywriter might have trouble adapting to selling office supplies. And go with your gut—if a writer shows samples you can't stop reading, he or she is probably a winner.

The Best Advertising Resources

If you need help creating a blockbuster advertising message, read any of these books. They're the best on the subject.

TRY IT HIS WAY

Allen Harpham is a computer consultant who believes in networking and volunteer work to build a client base. He got his first few customers by calling other consultants who were happy to give him business they were too busy to handle themselves. He maintained a good relationship with his former boss, who ended up giving him assignments. And his volunteer work for the chamber of commerce has led to a number of contacts that he eventually converted to customers. These are techniques that can work for any new business.

- *How to Make Your Advertising Twice as Effective at Half the Cost* by Herschell Gordon Lewis, published by Dartnell, 1992.

- *The Guerrilla Marketing Handbook* by Jay Levinson and Seth Godin, published by Houghton Mifflin, 1995.

- *Ogilvy on Advertising* by David Ogilvy, published by Random House, 1987.

THE 80/20 PROFIT RULE

It's a well-known scientific fact that 80 percent of your profits will come from 20 percent of your customers. That 20 percent is where you need to concentrate your efforts. Nurture their businesses, help them along. They're easy to ignore, because they're probably not the ones who do the griping, who need attention, who give you the headaches. But be careful not to take these big profit-making accounts for granted. Think about what characterizes these clients, and work on ways to get more of them. That's the way to help your business grow.

Direct Mail

Many start-up businesses have earned fortunes for their owners who marketed through direct mail. Direct mail is perfect for reaching very targeted markets, such as all motorcycle owners in five nearby zip codes. And you can measure the effectiveness of direct mail like no other form of marketing.

Even better, direct mail doesn't care whether you're giant or just a start-up. The cost of a direct mail campaign can be as little as a dollar—send three letters to three people!

On the downside, it's hard to close sales with direct mail. It's best used as an adjunct to other marketing means. For example, you may mail your real estate management clients a quarterly newsletter, in addition to calling on them in person every two months. The newsletter keeps you in their minds (especially if it contains useful information that your client looks forward to reading about) so that when you do call, they know who you are.

In quantity, however, stamps get expensive and unfortunately, most direct mail marketers waste a lot of them. Targeting your audience is the key to

getting the most out of your direct mail campaign. If you don't target your audience carefully, you almost guarantee that your mailing will not be cost-effective. You must know as much about your target audience as possible: age, gender, income, occupation, education, family size, and so on, before you begin a direct mail effort—that way you won't waste stamps sending letters to people who don't want to hear from you.

Mailing lists are the direct mailer's most valuable assets. You can rent very targeted lists from list brokers for around 10 cents a name. Look in the yellow pages or business-to-business listings to find brokers. Ask for their catalogs to see if they can offer just the list you need. But the best mailing list is one you build yourself. Use customer files, warranty service requests, frequent buyer plans, addresses culled from contest entries, and the like to build your own list from the day you start your business.

FIVE WAYS TO PROMOTE YOURSELF AS AN EXPERT

1. Hold a workshop.

2. Give a speech.

3. Write an article.

4. Produce a report.

5. Make an instructional videotape or audiotape.

Testing is the other key to a successful direct mail campaign. Mail 100 or 1,000 letters to a random cross section of your list. Based on the response, you can then fairly accurately predict the response you'll receive when you mail 100 times that many. Testing requires good recordkeeping, consistency (if you change your offer it will change the response rate), and patience. Test ads with different offers, different colors, and different headlines. Track responses by putting a code on each ad, by using slightly different wording, or by using a different telephone number or post office box for responses.

Copywriting for direct mail is different from other advertising. For one thing, you have much more room to work with. Many successful direct mail letters run several pages long. Instead of quick statements of benefits and features, they may launch into lengthy tales designed to tug at readers' heartstrings before finally arriving at the offer.

FOUR WAYS TO GET FREE RADIO PUBLICITY

1. Call your local station to give them interesting information about your market.

2. Supply your favorite morning show DJ with a joke.

3. Send a tray of breakfast pastries compliments of your business.

4. Send a radio station a testimonial about how you love to listen to a particular program.

Direct Mail Copywriting Golden Rules

Here are a few direct mail copywriting hints:

- Write personal letters. Make the letter as different from junk mail as you can. Handwrite the salutations and closings. Include a personal handwritten note on the bottom.

- Send to a name, never just a title or address. A letter mailed to "Dear Recipient" is much less likely to get read than one sent to "Dear John Baker."

- Use "Dear (first name)," for a salutation. This informality is acceptable and avoids confusing genders.

- In the first paragraph, say who referred you and how what you're offering will help your recipient.

- Get and use testimonials from persons famous and nonfamous advocating the use of your business or service.

- Ask for the sale. Never forget to request the order. If you don't ask the recipient to do something (like buy your product or service, call for more information, or take advantage of an offer you're making), then you've let a good opportunity go to waste.

- Make a special offer, such as a free cookbook to go with barbecue utensils you're selling.

- Make a limited-time offer to induce recipients to act now.

- Offer a guarantee if the product isn't satisfactory.

- Include a postscript—tests show the P.S. is one of the most read sections of a direct mail letter.

- Enclose other materials such as order forms, brochures, and testimonials.

Some of the best direct mail tools are also lowest in cost. Try mailing newsletters, postcards, and coupons alone or in combination with direct mail letters to achieve high-impact, low-outlay direct mail results.

Follow up by telephone, sales call, or additional mailings. As in other advertising, repetition counts in direct mail. One letter to 5,000 people rarely works as well as five letters, spread out over five months, to 1,000 people.

The Best Direct Mail Resources

There are a lot of resources out there for the direct mail marketer. Here are some of the best:

- *Direct Mail Copy That Sells* by Herschell Gordon Lewis, published by Prentice-Hall Trade, 1984.

- *The Golden Mailbox: How to Get Rich Direct Marketing Your Product* by Ted Nicholas, published by Upstart, 1992.

- *Do-It-Yourself Direct Marketing: Secrets for Small Business* by Mark S. Bacon, published by John Wiley & Sons, 1994.

THE FOUR Ps OF MARKETING

Marketing is more than advertising and sales. Organize your marketing strategy according to the well-known Four Ps:

1. Clearly identify your **Product.**

2. Let folks know the **Price.**

3. **Provide distribution channels** to get the product to your customers.

4. **Promote,** promote, promote.

- *Target Marketing for the Small Business: Researching, Reaching, and Retaining Your Target Market* by Linda Pinson and Jerry Jinnett, published by Dearborn Financial Publishing, Inc., 1996.

Telemarketing

Businesses spend more on marketing by telephone than any other medium. Odds are, you can market your business at least in part by using this uniquely powerful, flexible, personal, and ubiquitous tool.

Telemarketing comes in two types: incoming and outgoing. Outgoing calls are the kind that interrupt you and your family at dinner. Incoming is when you call to order or inquire about a product or service.

From your perspective as a business owner, taking incoming calls is better than making outgoing calls. Incoming callers are calling because they are already interested in what you have to sell and often ready to buy. Outgoing calls, on the other hand, have to be carefully targeted to be effective, and even then may be perceived as intrusive.

Incoming Telemarketing

Generating incoming calls is a job for your other promotional tools. If you put your telephone number on a billboard, include it in a newsletter, or get it printed in a newspaper article, you are going to generate some incoming calls.

Make it easy for callers to reach you by using a toll-free number. Try to get an easy-to-remember number, preferably one that spells something, such as

ALTERNATIVE ADVERTISING

Traditional advertising is expensive—a one-page four-color ad in a trade publication can run as much as $4,000 and ten times that much in a consumer publication. But there are less costly alternatives. Think about poster ads in airports, bus terminals, bus stops, and train stations, shopping carts, ski resorts, and commercials that run on supermarket TV monitors. All of these can be had for a fraction of the cost of big-time media, and pinpoint your audience, guerrilla-style.

555-KICK if you are running a karate school. And never miss an opportunity to spread your number around on ads, business cards, brochures, coupons, service manuals, and other promotional material. You've got to give people a reason to call you, of course. Offer a discount, a special offer, a free consultation, or even a privileged piece of information.

When you get an incoming call, make sure you handle it properly. Have enough lines and operators to avoid long waits on hold. Always answer the phone the same way, with a greeting and identification of the business—"Hello! Thanks for calling Spotless Maid Service." Get information about your caller, such as name, address, and phone number. Be friendly, but goal-oriented. Don't have a lengthy chat and hang up only to find you have no order, or any idea who called.

You might want to try hanging a mirror by your phone (you sound better when you smile), and it's also a good idea to tape your end of the phone call for a while. Reviewing these tapes will help you stamp out the ums, the aahs, and the fast-talking that many neophytes face when learning to talk on the phone professionally.

TRY IT HIS WAY

Svante Rodegard is a computer equipment exporter who believes in the power of building relationships to build sales. He spends lots of time on the phone just talking to people, asking about their families, and making friends. His no-pressure, low-key attitude has earned him respect in his market and a reputation for really caring about his clients' needs. In the long run, it's better to create a solid base of reliable, repeat customers than to make a few quick hits. It takes a little more effort, but it's much more rewarding—on a personal as well as a business level.

Outgoing Telemarketing

Outgoing telemarketing is different. Instead of your other promotional tools bringing people to you, you rely on carefully targeted calling lists to take you to them. Targeting is just as important for telemarketing as it is for direct mail, maybe even more so. If you're trying to sign up customers for your lawn care service, calling someone who lives in an apartment complex is a waste of your time and theirs. Know

TRY IT HIS WAY

Be sure to remember the folks you left behind when you go out on your own. Jeff Dinardo, of Dinardo Design, says 33 percent of his business comes from his former employer, Houghton Mifflin, the Boston-based publishing company. He was careful to maintain a good relationship with them and it paid off by enabling him to take on their projects when he started his company.

whom you need to be calling, in as much detail as possible, before you dial.

In fact, combining direct mail with telemarketing can often be a good idea. Once you've targeted a group, contact them with a direct mail letter, brochure, or catalog. Then follow up with a phone call. They'll already be somewhat familiar with your business, and discussion will flow more easily.

Rent or buy calling lists from the same list brokers who provide you with mailing lists. Often you can get the same list with or without phone numbers. Large, indiscriminate lists are used by boiler room operations, where low-paid marketers speed-dial numbers and spew broad-spectrum pitches. This isn't for you. As a small business person, you will probably want to boost your success rate—and reduce your overall costs—by carefully targeting both list and pitch to the right markets.

Scripts are written procedures for talking to telemarketing prospects. They are intended to help you explain benefits consistently and overcome standard objections on the way to a successful call. While there's no such thing as an all-purpose script, they do often have similarities—many of which they share with direct mail.

A script may make you uncomfortable, but if making money is your goal, you'd better get over it! Without a script, there's no way for you to edit yourself, no way for you to discover what works and what doesn't. Over time, you'll get so comfortable with your script it will be like you don't even have one—but it's worth the effort to write one.

Greet prospects by name, and to repeat their names frequently during the conversation. Make it clear that this is a business call, and identify yourself and your business. Say, "Hello, Mr. Smith, this is Robin Hood with Merry Men Uniforms."

A personal reference, a mailing in advance, or being able to reference an article that just ran in the local newspaper about your business or industry, may make a huge difference. Warm calls are 100 times better than cold ones. Here are some calling suggestions:

- Always mention who referred you (if someone did) and explain why you're calling. Build on previous contacts, as in, "You should have received a free coupon for a week's uniform rentals recently."

- Qualify the prospect with a question like, "Do you make your company's decisions about uniform rentals?"

- Stress the benefits of your product or service. Tell your potential customer how your product or service will make his life better or easier or happier.

- Avoid yes-or-no questions. Try to get the person you've called to reveal something about herself that will help you sell to her.

- Strive to continue the relationship more than close the sale by, for instance, making an appointment for an in-person sales call next week.

- Gather information to bulk up your mailing list and market information: "How many employees wear uniforms at this facility? What number should I dial to reach you directly?" When you've done what you can, hang up.

TRY IT HER WAY

Stevie Ann Rinehart is an illustrator whose company, Cardtoons, offers personalized greeting cards and stationery, announcements, and invitations featuring humorous cartoons. She says word of mouth gave her business a boost when she was just getting started. In addition to handing out business cards and brochures to everyone she knew, she did some work for free—work she wouldn't have gotten otherwise—in those early months when she wasn't overwhelmed with orders. This pro bono work ended up more than paying for itself when satisfied customers spread the word and generated genuine clients who rewarded her with repeat business. She's never regretted those first free jobs—she considers them free advertising.

TRY IT HER WAY

Testimonials—those nice things people say about you—are terrific sources of free advertising. Dawn Orford, a trade show consultant, finds out what her customers think of her work by sending surveys to each one after a job is finished. In addition to discovering ways to improve her service, she uses the positive comments in a testimonial flyer she sends to prospective clients.

- Show respect for the person's time. Make your point and make it up front.

Just as there's no all-purpose script, there's rarely a call that lets you follow your script perfectly. Keep it at hand to guide you. But use street smarts and think on your feet to make the most of any call. Here are some resources that might help:

- *Powerful Telephone Skills: A Quick and Handy Guide for Any Manager or Business Owner* by Editors of Career Press, published by Career Press, 1993.

- *Successful Telephone Selling in the '90's* by Martin D. Shafiroff and Robert L. Shook, published by HarperCollins, 1990.

Online Marketing

Online marketing is the black hole for most small businesses. You may find yourself spending time and money and getting nothing in return.

There are two critical things to remember when you go online to market:

1. E-mail gets read and gets directly to people, but *you must not send unsolicited mail*. Sending a letter to a list of strangers is called Spam, and sooner or later it will dramatically hurt your business.

2. The World Wide Web is like a trade show with more than 1,000,000 booths in it. Just putting up a booth is not going to get people to come look at it.

There are scores of books about what the Net is and how to use it. But if you keep the two rules above in mind, you'll discover that:

- The currency of the Web is permission. Get permission to write to someone, to e-mail him, and you've just made a huge step toward turning him into a customer.

- Do for others before you ask them to do for you. By giving first, you gain trust and respect online.

- Online commerce is about to happen. If you can come up with unique products, sold in a fun way, you may be on your way.

- Don't spend more than $5,000 on your Web site until you know that it's going to pay off. And if you do invest in a Web site, you'd better invest in some other marketing methods that drive traffic to your site.

TRY IT HER WAY

Linda Abraham promoted her résumé and college application editing and writing service by giving lectures and writing a pamphlet on how to do it yourself. The result of these efforts was that she created a reputation for herself as a professional and the person to call if you're looking for help writing your personal history.

Personal Selling

Nothing happens until somebody makes a sale, and the personal sales call remains the leading promotional tool for many small businesses. Why? Because it's the most individualized kind of promotion and the personal touch is the small business's strong suit. When you show up on a prospect's doorstep to tell about the great new kid's computer game you developed, it's as personal as you can get. And you can bet Bill Gates isn't going to take that kind of time with each one of his customers.

Not every product or service is ideal for personal selling. Low-margin, high-volume consumer items are poor examples. It's not worth your time to try to buttonhole every shopper walking into the local supermarket to try to get them to buy a bottle of your all-natural salsa (although it might be a good idea once in a while as part of a word-of-mouth campaign).

On the other hand, costly and complicated services and products, especially those sold business-to-business, are usually best promoted personally. It's not likely a newspaper ad could convince a Fortune 500 company to hire your start-up to provide catering services for its local office. But if you could get 15 minutes with the head of regional purchasing, you might be able to swing it.

What makes a good salesperson? First off, you've got to believe. Second, you've got to be a master of the skills that help you overcome the inclination that most people have to distrust strangers. And third, you've got to have patience. Here are three more great qualities for any salesperson to have:

- *Discipline.* It's not easy to keep making sales calls when rejection seems inevitable. Good salespeople do, and can organize and execute systematic sales presentations and strategies as well.

- *Initiative.* Most salespeople work with relatively little direct oversight; many are out of the office most of the time. A good salesperson is self-motivated and energetic. The best recognize no clock, seeking contacts at and away from work.

- *Principles.* A salesperson is an agent of your company. Any representation a salesperson makes reflects directly on you. It only makes sense to hire salespeople of unquestioned integrity.

TRY IT HER WAY

Jan Melnik owns Comprehensive Services, Plus, a secretarial services and consulting company. She offers discounts to clients who refer new customers, a policy she says has resulted in a lot of new business.

Closing the Sale

Although countless books have been written about personal selling, it can be boiled down to six steps.

1. *Qualify.* Qualify your prospect to make sure he or she controls the decision to buy. Influencers are a step down from decision-makers, but can

also be powerful. If you're selling energy-saving lighting systems and can get the architects for a new building to write specifications around your product, it may be as effective as signing the building owner to a long-range bulb contract.

2. *Contact.* Put yourself in front of your prospect, whether it's through a formal appointment or a chance meeting in the parking lot of a local restaurant. It may seem obvious, but many salespeople fail because they just don't contact enough prospects.

3. *Question.* Find out what your prospect's needs are. Obvious assumptions may be wrong. Your architect may be avid for any kind of energy savings when you think he or she is only interested in cutting costs. If you can find out what your prospect needs, then it's a lot easier to sell him what you have.

4. *Seek objections.* Objections are a salesperson's best friend. If you can get your prospect to tell you why she won't buy, then you can target your sales pitch to overcome the objection.

5. *Ask for it.* In personal selling, your objective is to get the sale now. Asking for the order, even if temporarily unsuccessful, keeps your sales call on track. Ask, "Mr. Architect, if I show how you can put these energy-saving lights in and save your client money long-term, would you write these specs in today?" A "yes" means you can get the sale now. A "no" means you have more objections to uncover and overcome.

6. *Get it.* Have a pen and order form (filled out as you talk) handy. When your close gets an oral "yes," make it official by getting it in writing.

TRY IT HIS WAY

A publicity campaign should be consistent and persistent. Don't be afraid of overselling. Jeff Mayer is an executive organization consultant who called and sent press releases to his media contacts once a month. His efforts finally paid off when a reporter wrote a story on corporate organizing and quoted Jeff, calling him the industry expert.

TRY IT HER WAY

Ilise Benun is a self-promo-
tion and marketing consultant based in Hoboken, New
Jersey. Her quarterly
newsletter, *The Art of Self-
Promotion*, is really a means
to publicize her business,
but she makes the most of
it by selling it. She does mail
it free to members of the
press and suggests they
reprint any of it at no charge
as long as they give her
credit. This has proved to be
a smart move—she's been
quoted all over as an expert
in her field and she's gotten
consulting jobs as a result.

Some of the greatest marketing minds have written the best books about selling on the market.
Here are some of the best:

- *Ziglar on Selling* by Zig Ziglar, published by Thomas Nelson, 1991.

- *Selling the Dream: How to Promote
  Your Product, Company, or Ideas—And
  Make a Difference—Using Everday
  Evangelism* by Guy Kawasaki, pub-
  lished by Harperbusiness, 1992.

- *Secrets of Closing the Sale* by Zig Ziglar,
  published by Berkley Publishing
  Group, 1985.

Publicity

Publicity stands out among promotional tools for
two reasons: It's (almost) free and it's uniquely
effective. Getting your product, service, or business
(or yourself) mentioned in a magazine that gets tens of thousands of dollars for a single
ad may require no more than a stamp, envelope, and sheet of paper for a short news
release. In fact, most editorial mentions are not for sale at any price. When your new in-
home pet shampoo service leads the local evening news, you've done something the
biggest TV advertiser in the land can't necessarily duplicate. Plus, studies have shown
that even noncommittal mentions in an article or newscast imply an endorsement and
are highly effective at swaying consumers. If you're lucky enough to get an outright
plug from a reviewer or other opinion leader, you've struck promotional gold.

Remember that the media has a job to do, and that there's a real shortage of interesting stories. That's one reason why everything you read seems so alike. If you can make
it easy, they're going to write about it. In fact, one study showed that 80 percent of
all articles were "placed" by a PR person or entrepreneur!

At the same time, publicity does have its limits. The main one is control. You can write a radio spot's copy yourself, and specify exactly when and where it will appear. But the radio reporter who covered your grand opening may mention it in a ten-second blurb that runs at 2:00 a.m.—mispronouncing your name—or may not use it at all. You have to take the good with the bad in publicity.

Your Publicity Plan

There are tens of thousands of media outlets in the United States, employing hundreds of thousands of editors, producers, writers, broadcasters, and others. Without a plan, you could easily exhaust your energy and patience without reaching a single one effectively. Your plan need not be complicated. Planning for publicity can involve as little as asking and answering just two questions:

The first question is, "What do you hope to accomplish?" Publicity is best at boosting name recognition and establishing credibility. It's not dependable at generating actual calls and letters. Of course, always make sure you include your contact info so readers and listeners know how to get in touch with you. A good publicity goal for the operator of a bed and breakfast, for example, might be to make her business's name more familiar to travel agents in a nearby large city.

Your next question is, "What's the best way to do that?" In the B&B owner's case, a mention in a feature article in the travel section of the big-city daily sounded good. Looking further, she saw the paper's travel editor mentioned the upcoming publication of a directory of regional B&Bs. So, the owner mailed off her brochure and a press release to the editor and ended up getting mentioned in a regional travel newspaper article and was offered a listing in the B&B directory.

TRY IT HER WAY

When you send press releases, target your mailings to the publications that are most relevant to your business and try to narrow them even further to the people you know. Kimberly Stanséll, a business information specialist, does just that, and she says her response rate is three times higher than when she mass-mailed her releases to everyone and anyone.

TRY IT HER WAY

When you contact prospective clients or existing customers to stay in touch, try to find ways you can help them. Marcia Layton, a business plan writer, calls on financial consultants, bankers, lawyers, and venture capitalists. If a client is looking for capital, she provides a real service by sending summaries of that business plan to capital sources at no charge. It's an effective way to keep her company and her name out there, and she says she has gotten new business from these sales calls disguised as favors.

It's not always that easy, however. It's rare to have your first press release generate a news story. You often need to sell the media on the newsworthiness of your business in the same way you need to sell your customers on the value of your product. And you use many of the same methods to do it. Here are the three basic rules for generating publicity:

1. *Target your market.* Sound familiar? You need to target the media you want to reach. The B&B owner above sent her press release to the travel editor of her local paper. The same release sent to *Time* magazine, or even to the city desk editor at the local paper, would have been a wasted effort. Pick out the five or ten media outlets that already cover businesses like yours and focus on getting them to cover you.

2. *Make your press release count.* Quantity is important with regard to press releases, but quality is even more important. Make sure your release is newsworthy. There has to be a reason why you're sending it and a compelling story behind it. The B&B owner above sent out one press release when she opened her new in-ground pool, and another when she changed the rates on her rooms, and a third after a local celebrity spent the weekend in the master suite.

3. *Be persistent.* If you send out one release to hundreds of media outlets and then sit back and wait, the chances of getting covered are slim to none. Remember to treat the media just like a prospective client. Keep yourself in the local newspaper editor's mind and one day, when he needs a story to run, he'll think of you. It's always better to send five press releases to 20 highly targeted media outlets over the course of five months than it is to

send out one release to 100 random outlets just once. Don't give up.

Press releases are the basic tools of the publicist. They are brief memos that describe your business's newsworthy aspects, and invite editors, producers, and others to cover you. Writing and sending out press releases effectively is a valuable skill.

Before you ever put a word of your release on paper, you have to know where you are going to send it. Time frames govern your selection to a large degree. So does the extent of the appeal you can offer.

Want coverage for a local celebrity making a promotional appearance at your new hair salon next week? A local newspaper or broadcast station is your best hope. Many magazines have lead times from three months to a year or more. That means if you want something in your local city monthly about your personal shopping service for Christmas gift-givers, you had better make your pitch no later than October 1.

TRY IT HIS WAY

The secret to Panther Advertising and Marketing's success is the two free weeks owner Scott Bruce gives his customers at the beginning of their relationship. Some people might treat these meetings as sales calls—for which you don't get paid anyway—but Scott uses this time to really get to know his prospective clients' needs and expectations. At the end of the period, he's able to come up with a custom-made advertising and marketing proposal. By the time he's delivered that proposal, he's already established himself as an integral part of that customer's business and he rarely loses a sale.

And be reasonable about your story's appeal: What's important to you may not be to a journalist. If you haven't seen a particular media outlet cover an event or issue like the one you're proposing, chances are it won't start now.

Subject matter is also a concern. Trade journals that cover your specific industry may be easy sells. General interest magazines, newspapers, and broadcast news organizations are tougher. However, many general interest outlets have regular segments, columns, or pages devoted to narrower topics. Your expertise as a video-camera store-owner may bore the front-page editor at your local paper, but fascinate the columnist who writes the "Electronic Hobbies" column every Saturday.

Writing a press release is a straightforward project. They even have a standard format that guides you (and controls you—if you vary from it much, your release may be viewed with disdain). Here are major elements:

TRY IT HIS WAY

Chris Beal, who sells used computers, uses a low-cost posting service to get flyers on college campuses all over the country.

- *Length.* Two or three double-spaced, typed pages is enough for a typical news release. It has to be a quick read since many news outlets get dozens a day. If you have a lot more to tell, try splitting it into two releases, sent a couple of weeks apart. This will help build name recognition among media contacts while minimizing their investment in reading any one release. Use letterhead for the first page, plain paper for the remaining ones.

- *Headline.* The most important part of your press release is the headline. Make it compelling. Most of the ones that cross your local editor's desk (and there could be hundreds each week) are tedious and boring. If yours isn't, it's much more likely to get picked up. Your headline should be short—about seven words is right—and about a third of the way down the first page. It should succinctly summarize the most important points of your release. "Local Architect Selected to Historic Preservation Board" is a good example for a local paper. But if you're trying to get into *Time* magazine, your headline must be geared toward the reader. For example, "Scientists Clone Sheep: Are Your Children Next?"

- *Contact.* Few news outlets will print or broadcast a story from a release without checking out the facts and fleshing out the details. Put your name and phone number just above or below the headline, and perhaps again at the end of the release. If you're hard to reach, provide a pager, cellular phone, or e-mail address. Reporters often want to move fast when they're interested.

- *Date.* Old news is no news and a release without a date is apt to be discarded out of hand. Always put the current date.

- *Dateline.* The dateline tells the city, state, or country where the news is happening. This is of crucial importance to local editors and producers. Type the city and state where you are, followed by a dash, before starting the first sentence of the text. For example: "Washington, DC—Beltway computer shoppers today got their first look at next Christmas's hottest PC accessory..."

- *Lead.* This is the first and most important paragraph. It should summarize the release in no more than 40 words. Cover the Five Ws: who, what, when, where, and why. As in: "Local architect John Smith (who) was today (when) named to the Historical Preservation Board (what) for Jones County (where) in recognition of his 'excellent and standard-setting work' on restoring older homes (why), board President Joe Jones said." In 33 words, this imparts the news.

TRY IT HIS WAY

Robert Pizzo is an illustrator who gets the most out of his advertising and promotion dollars. He designed his direct mail piece to fit in a letter-size envelope and he stuffs it in every envelope he mails. In addition, he makes reprints of an ad he runs in an annual design directory and sends this along. You can mail these with invoices, letters, proposals, and other correspondence to make the most of every mailing.

The rest of the release is up for grabs. You may want to organize it very plainly, taking a paragraph to elaborate on each of the Five Ws. At the very end provide one or two paragraphs of details on you and your company. It's also a good idea to specifically say that you are available for interviews.

Include a few direct quotations in your words or those of another person in your company. Enclose them in quotation marks, put "Mr. Smith says" or the equivalent after each. Write what you want for your own quotes but say them out loud a few times to see if they sound natural.

Finally, make the release's packaging attention-grabbing. Attach a handwritten personal note for the reporter or editor. Enclose a sample of your product if it's

TRY IT HIS WAY

Stew Reads is a toy industry public relations pro who
puts his extensive knowl-
edge of the industry to good
use. He takes what he
knows and converts it to
goodwill by publishing a
monthly newsletter that he
distributes to potential and
actual clients. They're grate-
ful for all the free insider
information about new products, personnel changes,
and hot sellers, and he's
able to keep his name in his
customers' faces in a way
they appreciate.

appropriate. Do something slightly wacky—a
news release wrapped around a foam baseball will
draw attention while it highlights the seasonal discount your print shop is offering on uniform
silkscreening to local youth teams.

Sales Promotions and Other Marketing Tools

Other promotional tools include everything from
in-store displays and frequent customer giveaways
to trade show demonstrations and campaigns to
generate word of mouth. Just because they're not
so easily categorized, don't think these are less
important than other promotional tools. Frequent
flyer clubs revolutionized airline marketing almost
on their own, and word of mouth, though little
recognized, is one the most muscular promotional
tools available. There are an infinite number of
marketing ideas for every small business. Here are
some ideas to begin with, all of which can be
tailor-made for your start-up:

- *Comarketing.* If you can convince a local pizza restaurant to carry a small
rack of the videos you rent, you're in good shape to help the pizzeria while
helping yourself, and at very little added cost. Many other businesses have
done the same, from credit cards that offer discounts on car rentals to
amusement parks that print coupons for cut-rate tickets on soft drink cans.
Look constantly for ways you can comarket with other small businesses.

- *Customer service.* Top-flight customer service made Nordstrom department stores a unique name in retailing (even though they carry much the
same stuff as other stores). In that sense, service is a promotional tool.
Wow your customers with service and chances are they'll be back—and
even more importantly, they'll tell their friends about you.

- *Demonstrations.* Seeing is believing. Tools, cleaning liquids, and kitchen gadgets are just a few of the products that have been introduced to the markets primarily by in-person demonstrations at stores, fairs, expositions, and even street corners. Any time you can personally demonstrate your product or service, especially if it represents a new concept, you are promoting effectively.

- *Free samples and giveaways.* Many small software companies got their start with shareware—working programs distributed on the honor system for which users are expected to pay only if they prove useful. Similar sampling strategies have been used to launch countless products and services. While sampling isn't always inexpensive, and can be abused by unscrupulous consumers, it's a time-tested promotional tool with great promise for many kinds of businesses.

- *Frequent buyer plans.* Airlines have been joined by bookstores, grocery stores, hotels, long-distance telephone companies, and many others in using this loyalty-building tool. It's most appropriate when you are dealing in a commodity, largely indistinguishable from what others are offering (like long-distance service or best-selling books). One pet supply store owner offers customers a free 40-pound bag of dog food after they've purchased nine bags.

- *In-store displays.* Many buying decisions are made on impulse, as a distinctive display rack catches the shopper's eye. And, it's worth adding, many stores refuse to carry products that don't provide some kind of in-store display. It can range from a complete shelving system to a simple cardboard sign that stands

TRY IT HIS WAY

There are ways to act big even if you're small. One way is to reach customers all over the country by phone and e-mail. Take a hint from Bob Westenberg, whose direct mail/advertising business prospered thanks to his ingenuity. He had personal relationships with his clients even though he did little traveling and they were scattered throughout the country. When they renewed their yearly ads, he would thank them by arranging to pay for a dinner at a restaurant near them. It was a thoughtful gesture his customers appreciated and repaid with repeat business.

TRY IT HER WAY

Use the small size of your business to be flexible about operating hours. Pattianne Turner, who owns Computer Aided Services & Training, makes herself available to talk to clients in the evenings and on weekends. Since many of her customers are shopping for printed materials for weddings and other events, they appreciate being able to reach her after normal business hours, and she finds she picks up more business because they're more relaxed and have more time to talk.

on the floor. But it's becoming increasingly important in the distribution and sale of all kinds of products.

- *Networking.* Everybody networks to some extent but few do it effectively. To excel at networking, select the groups, activities, and meetings you'll network in carefully, making sure that your target audience is well-represented there. Get involved rather than just going to meetings. A computer consultant who serves on her chamber of commerce's high-tech committee is far more likely to get business out of it than one who just eats lunch, listens to the speech, and leaves.

- *Testimonials and celebrity endorsements.* Obtaining an endorsement from a respected public figure can turn a small business into a large one virtually overnight. Choose the right celebrity, one with clout in your target market and one you can afford. For most businesses, that means obtaining referrals from local or lesser luminaries, or even believable testimonials from unknowns. But one small skate maker used a combination of royalties and equity to sign hockey superstar Wayne Gretzky as an endorser of its products, generating millions of dollars in sales.

- *Trade shows.* Trade shows exist for almost any product, service or industry. Go to the right one and you'll find a unique concentration of the most important movers and shakers in yours. Trade shows can be expensive, however, so attend as a visitor before laying out the cash to exhibit.

- *Word of mouth.* Many sales are consummated solely on the strength of a personal referral. For some businesses, such as doctors, attorneys, and dentists, personal referrals comprise virtually all their marketing promotion. You can start positive word of mouth by simply asking customers to tell a friend about you.

The Power of Promotional Creativity

One of a start-up's strengths is its freedom from the past. Other companies may have "we don't do it that way" restrictions. Don't limit your promotions by more than your imagination and judgment. Anything you can think of that will inform, persuade, or remind can be an effective promotion.

Where to Learn More

- *Do-It-Yourself Advertising: How to Produce Great Ads, Brochures, Catalogs, Direct Mail, and Much More* by Fred E. Hahn, published by John Wiley & Sons, 1993.

- *1001 Ways to Market Yourself and Your Small Business* by Lisa Shaw, published by Peregrine, 1997.

- *The One to One Future: Building Relationships One Customer at a Time* by Don Peppers and Martha Rogers, Ph.D., published by Bantam/Doubleday Dell Publishers, 1997.

- *Guerrilla Marketing Online: The Entrepreneur's Guide to Earning Profits on the Internet* by Jay Conrad Levinson and Charles Rubin, published by Houghton Mifflin, 1995. The guerrilla marketing guru teams up with an online expert to produce a comprehensive guide to marketing your business on the Internet and with online services.

TRY IT HIS WAY

Before you mail an expensive printed piece, increase its chances of getting read. Management consultant Antonio Nuñez always sends a cover letter mentioning a mutual acquaintance. "Jim Culhane suggested I send this to you..." Of course, he's cleared it with Culhane first, an act of courtesy and an opportunity for a subtle sales pitch, too.

- *The Market Planning Guide* by David H. Bangs, Jr., published by Upstart Publishing Company, 1994.

- American Association of Advertising Agencies (AAAA), 405 Lexington Ave., 18th Floor, New York, NY 10174, (212) 682-2500. 4As, as it's known, can refer you to a reputable ad agency in your area.

- *Positioning: The Battle for Your Mind* by Al Ries and Jack Trout, published by Warner Books, 1993. One of the seminal marketing books, describing how to position your product or service in the marketplace.

EXPANDING *the* BUSINESS

CHAPTER TEN

There's more to growth than meets the eye. If you have the opportunity or just the **desire** to expand your start-up business, you'll need to know when, how, and why to do it if you're to make the most of the chance.

Most businesses don't grow very big. If you take a look at the Census Bureau's list of all U.S. businesses, you'll see 180,000 with multiple business units, five million that have only a single establishment, and nearly 14 million one-person businesses.

Why do so many stay small? It's not easy to generate the added sales necessary to grow. But it's also true that bigger isn't always better. Many entrepreneurs start businesses solely to avoid having to work for someone else. And, in fact, staying small isn't a bad option. Growth has some built-in problems.

You and your employees may be overwhelmed by new responsibilities in a larger enterprise. You may be the best cake-decorator in town, and you may do fine managing your sister-in-law and best friend, who are working part-time making deliveries. But if you hire three more cake decorators (including two trainees), a full-time delivery person, someone to answer the phone, and a part-time bookkeeper, you will have to deal with absenteeism, benefits, vacations, and all the other issues of an employer. You may find your management skills overtaxed and the added stress of having to pay all of those salaries a real energy drain.

TRY IT HER WAY

Referrals are the cornerstones of building new businesses. Bonnie Wallsh is a meeting planner who thinks referrals are so valuable, she's willing to pay for them. She asks clients, vendors, friends, and meeting attendees for recommendations and offers a finder's fee for any new business someone sends her way—sometimes as much as 15 percent of her own fee. She says it's been worth it. She's turned Bonnie Wallsh & Associates into a successful business and she believes referrals have played a large part.

You'll almost certainly find it more difficult to communicate with the people in your expanded workforce. When your custom hardwood flooring company consists of just you, a supervisor, and two crews, it takes a five-minute meeting for you to inform everybody of the need to put in some overtime next month. If you add a new office in the next city, two more crews, and two new supervisors, you're going to have to hold a couple of meetings and cope with travel time, schedule conflicts, and other hassles every time you need to pass the word on something.

It will be tough to maintain team spirit and cohesiveness. When it's just you and your partner running a tax-preparation office, you both know what you want and are motivated to accomplish it. But what does that new receptionist know of your dreams? And will franchisees sign on to your go-go spirit of competitiveness—or write you off as a workaholic?

Work may simply not be as exciting in a larger enterprise as when you were tiny and struggling. People are much the same from one company and one industry to

another, so the management challenges you face when your small business grows aren't likely to be as unique or interesting as when you were small and on the firing line every day. You may get bored.

If the challenges posted by growth don't seem interesting to you, small may be best. On the other hand, you may relish the prospect of tackling unfamiliar problems and mastering new skills. If so, you'll be happy to know there are also some very good reasons to grow.

Bigger companies can get increased economies of scale, leading to higher profits with relatively low added expense. If you run a printing company, your main expenses are the cost of your presses and the salaries of your employees. If you can run those presses an extra eight hours a day by adding a second shift, your profits are liable to rise sharply. Bigger companies may also find it easier to find financing, fight off rivals, develop new products and technologies, and withstand economic downturns.

Even for a company that could benefit by being bigger, growth at the wrong time can cause more trouble than it's worth. You may even commit a serious error by, for instance, choosing to grow in a shrinking market. If you borrow heavily to expand your gift shop into the vacant space next door just before the city decides to tear up the road in front of you for six months, the combination of higher debt payments and lower sales may unwrap your business prematurely.

How Do You Know When to Grow?

There are some key signs that may suggest your company would be better bigger.

When customers are banging on your door, their demands going unmet, you may need to add customer service and production capacity to hang onto them. A downtown florist who finds himself turning down lots of calls from suburban would-be customers would be well-advised to look into opening a branch in the burbs. Otherwise, those customers may stop calling, and tell others to do the same.

When employees (and you) are complaining of overwork and burnout, consider hiring people to reduce the workload. Overtired workers make mistakes. Employees who put in too much overtime start calling in sick. Entrepreneurs who get burned out make poor decisions. They may fail or sell their businesses and flee. If you don't have the enthusiasm you once had for a new shipment of floor coverings, maybe it's time to get some help in your Oriental rug store.

TRY IT HIS WAY

Chris Nowak is the founder of Rocky Mountain Motorworks, a distributor of parts for German cars. He has inspired confidence in his products by offering every customer a lifetime warranty on all parts. He minimizes his risk by returning defective parts to his suppliers. Although they balked at first, they soon realized that the increase in sales was worth the extra effort to make a quality product.

When you constantly find yourself being overpowered by much larger rivals, perhaps you'll need to match their bulk to compete effectively. Bigger is likely to be better in mature industries, such as automobile manufacturing, than in fast-growing, young ones such as computer game design. Indeed, in many immature markets, smaller, more nimble companies have an edge. Common sense, plus your individual business and industry needs, must guide you here. Your weekly shopper newspaper may benefit by judiciously expanding to a new city. But it could be a mistake for a literary agent to take on any and all authors who send manuscripts.

There are only so many ways to grow: increasing productivity, adding employees, adding products and services, adding space or locations, franchising or licensing, and entering new businesses are the main ones. Some businesses will be able to grow significantly by only using one, while others may have to employ a mix. Study these mechanisms of growth to find the ones that will yield the most results with the least risk.

Increasing Productivity

Growing doesn't always mean building new factories and hiring new workers. You may be able to significantly increase your output without adding a single employee, piece of equipment, or hour at the office by simply working smarter instead of harder. Many businesses find that the best way to grow, especially in the early stages of

expansion, is by streamlining procedures, automating processes, computerizing, training, and motivating employees.

Streamlining procedures means cutting out jobs that duplicate work done elsewhere, could be combined with another task, or are simply unnecessary. If your college guidance counseling service meets with clients once to assess their academic needs and again to measure their financial resources, you may be able to cut your meeting load in half by combining the interviews. That could free up enough resources to substantially grow your caseload.

Automating the tasks handled by steelworkers, refinery employees, sewing machine operators, and many other manufacturing employees has drastically cut these industries' needs for labor, while allowing them to actually increase output. You don't have to be U.S. Steel to do the same. A pizza place that installs Caller ID, so employees know who's calling before they pick up the phone, can significantly cut the time to process a take-out order, freeing up employees to deal with walk-in customers, cook pizzas, or take additional phone orders.

Computerize your business whenever and wherever it makes sense. Computers won't cure all ills. But if you're balancing the books, figuring the payroll, and managing inventory at your bagel shop with a pencil and paper, you could almost certainly free up many hours of your own time weekly by typing the data into inexpensive accounting software running on a plain-Jane PC. Even better—capture data automatically with computerized cash registers, electronic time clocks, and an electronic ordering system networked to your PC.

Training and motivating employees is an excellent way to handle growth without adding cost and complexity. A one-day course in using time management software for salespeople at a small women's apparel company could easily help sales grow without adding a single new product or employee.

Adding Employees

As your business grows, sooner or later you will find yourself adding employees. While hiring good people is no cinch (see chapter eight), adding workers is a good way to improve service, add expertise, and increase production fairly quickly. If you work in a personal services industry, such as a wedding consultant, there may be no way to expand without new employees.

Lousy service is one of the best indicators of a need to grow. And one of the easiest and fastest ways to improve service is to hire employees. More people can help you answer the phone faster, stay open later, turn around orders more quickly, and generally keep customers happier.

Adding employees can also let you increase output by working double shifts without buying more equipment or space. This is especially valuable for businesses that have sizable investments in fixed production assets. If you have sunk a lot of money into a new, specially padded truck for your business moving antiques, artwork, and delicate electronic instruments, the more you can keep that truck working, the sooner you can get it paid off. If you hire a new driver and loading team to work weekends and nights, you may be able to afford a third truck far sooner.

Part-time, seasonal, temporary, and contingent workers are used by almost 95 percent of companies, according to a study by Olsten national temp agency. If you have wide seasonal fluctuations in your business—like a fireworks display producer or a Christmas-only retailer—you probably already use temps and seasonal workers. Other firms can use contingent workers to expand rapidly to meet short-term, unexpected demand, then shrink when the crush is past.

The decision to hire new employees can't be made casually. New workers need lots of things other than paychecks. Each one adds to training costs, payroll bookkeeping, and management commitments. They'll need equipment, uniforms, tools, and space in which to work. It's easy to bring on a new salesman in your telemarketing firm, but if you have to build and equip a new office or cubicle, string a new phone line, and conduct a new training program, costs can mount rapidly.

Adding Products and Services

Henry Ford started out selling one car in one color. Today Ford Motor makes a rainbow of 70 vehicles under the Aston Martin, Ford, Jaguar, Lincoln, and Mercury labels.

Adding new (or variants of existing) products and services lets Ford reach new markets and raise sales without selling simply more of the same items. You can do the same.

Line extensions are good ways to grow. These are products or services that are related to existing produces and services. If you find your handmade vanilla-scented beeswax candles are selling extremely well, you may wish to extend the line by adding floral and spice scents. This kind of expansion is lower in risk than deciding to, say, sell flashlight batteries.

Cannibalization is a risk in any scheme to add new products that are related to ones you're already carrying. People who once bought your vanilla candles may now simply buy spice instead. This can be a zero-sum game (or worse) for the business owner, who pays for developing and producing a new product without getting higher overall sales in return. Plan line extensions carefully to minimize cannibalization.

You can eliminate cannibalization by introducing new products that are unrelated to existing ones. If you're formulating environmentally friendly pool chemicals, you could safely come up with a new chemical for treating drinking water without affecting your pool business. You can use the machinery, trucks, and employees you've acquired for your pool business, and likely sell to some of your existing customers on the strength of your established name.

Entering a new product arena becomes risky when it's too far afield of the business where you have a track record. Going from pool chemicals to, say, solutions for cleaning the tiles on the space shuttle won't allow you to use many of your existing resources.

Adding More Space or Locations

Retailers, wholesalers, shippers, manufacturers, and others who deal in physical goods need to be close to their markets and sources of supply. So adding new stores, warehouses, and factories can be an important way of growing for these businesses. And any growing business will eventually need added space, whether in its original location or a new one, in order to house its growing workforce or inventory.

Opening a new location is less costly and complicated than opening your first location. But it's still a decision to be made carefully. You'll have costs for rent,

Small Business Innovative Research (SBIR) Program

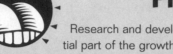

Research and development (R&D) is an essential part of the growth and expansion of any business. It enables you to find new markets and products, and compete more effectively.

The Small Business Innovative Development Act established SBIR in 1982, and it mandates ten federal departments and agencies to reserve a portion of their R&D funds to award to small businesses. These offices are:

• Department of Agriculture

• Department of Commerce

• Department of Defense

• Department of Education

• Department of Energy

• Department of Health and Human Services

• Department of Transportation

• Environmental Protection Agency

• National Aeronautics and Space Administration

• National Science Foundation

To receive an SBIR award or grant, you need to submit a proposal which will be judged on its degree of innovation, technical merit, and future market potential. Businesses that succeed in getting SBIR money receive it in two phases:

1. *Phase I.* Awards of up to $100,000 for a six-month feasibility study

2. *Phase II.* Two years of actual R&D work supported by awards up to $750,000

For more information about the SBIR program, contact:

U.S. Small Business Administration Office of Technology
409 Third St. SW
Washington, DC 20416
(202) 205-6450

Or visit the SBIR Web site at: http://www.sba.gov/sbir

improvements, deposits, inventory, equipment, packing, shipping, and more. Subject this decision to the same process you used in deciding where, when, and whether to open your first location.

You can expand cheaply by several methods. One of the most popular is to take over neighboring space. If your business is growing, scope out the leases of tenants next to you. Find out who's staying and who's leaving. If something looks like it will become available, begin negotiating with the landlord ahead of time. This technique minimizes costs for rent, deposits, utility connections, and moving.

If you can't expand locally, try to avoid moving your entire business to a larger location. Relocating lock, stock, and barrel means shutting your business down during the move, and downtime can get expensive. Try splitting your organization along natural fault lines by, for instance, keeping headquarters and administration in the original location and opening a new, separate facility for production or warehousing.

You may be able to expand a retail operation inexpensively by using small kiosks or mobile stands. If you need added space for office workers, try having some people work from their homes all or part of the day or obtain temporary, fully-equipped space in an office suite operation. When the growth appears to be long lasting, you can commit to permanent quarters.

Franchising

You may be able to get someone else to expand your business for you by franchising. McDonald's, 7-Eleven, H&R Block, and Radio Shack base their success on franchising. It's worked for a lot of other people, too. The International Franchise Association says about a third of all retail sales in the United States are funneled through more than a half-million franchised outlets.

A franchiser sells the right to start and run a business under a recognized name using preset business practices. The franchiser (you) gets to expand more rapidly and less expensively than if he did it all himself. The payoff comes in the form of a franchise fee paid to the franchiser, plus a royalty consisting of a percentage of all franchisees' sales. In exchange, the franchisee gets your help, trademarks, and other benefits.

Not all businesses franchise well. The best have a highly effective, comprehensive, and well-documented system of operation, including marketing, hiring, training, production, site selection, and financial management. You must be able to train other business people in running their businesses the same way you do. Your seafood restaurant may be highly successful, but if you can't tell somebody else how to achieve the same success, you aren't a good franchise candidate.

Franchising can be a low-cost, highly effective way of expanding for many businesses. But it has risks and obstacles. Strict regulation of franchisers means you will have lots of papers (prepared by expensive attorneys) to file in any state where you seek franchisees. It can be difficult to maintain control over the quality, pricing, and other aspects of franchisee operations. Rebellious franchisees could even wrest control of your business concept away from you.

Licensing

Licensing is another low-cost way to grow. It's an agreement by one company to let another use its trademarks, patents, proprietary technology, trade secrets, copyrights, or other valuable property. In exchange, you (the licenser) get a one-time fee or royalties on sales of products or services made or marketed under the license.

A license can involve anything from the rights to print a cartoon character's face to running a business under the same name as yours (franchising is a kind of licensing). Your software start-up might license to Microsoft to include your new technology for searching the World Wide Web in the next version of Internet Explorer. Or your custom upholstery company might license its secret refinishing technique to another upholsterer.

By tapping into the resources of existing companies, licensing can let you expand to new markets or ramp up production more quickly than you would otherwise. Ideally, you can simply sit back and collect the licensing checks as others do all the work and take all the risks. However, it usually takes oversight to ensure that licensees are maintaining quality standards and sticking to the terms of the license. The value of the new cartoon character you created for your comic strip might be harmed if a licensee began printing poor-quality T-shirts.

Entering New Businesses

Sometimes growth opportunities in your business are limited. You may see, based on the trend of declining births at local hospitals, that the number of children available to enter your dance academy will inevitably shrink in the next several years. Unless something looks likely to turn the trend around, it makes sense for you to enter a completely new business.

There are a couple of different strategies for entering new businesses. You can vertically integrate your existing business. This involves entering businesses that are further up or down the supply chain from where you are. A bookstore owner who decides to start publishing her own books is vertically integrating. So is a small publisher who decides to open a retail bookstore. Vertically integrating provides economies of scale, avoids paying middlemen, and lets you apply your experience to a similar occupation.

You can also enter an unrelated line of business, but that's certainly more difficult. You have to start over essentially from scratch, except that you will have the experience of your first business behind you.

The main advantage to being in two or more different lines of business is that it lets you protect yourself from unfavorable market or economic trends. This works best when you invest in businesses that are unrelated or counter-cyclical. A cigar store owner who is concerned that her smokes may fall out of favor with health-minded consumers might decide to start a fitness club so that she can profit no matter which way the fashion goes.

The cheapest way get into a new business is to do what you've already done: Start a new company. However, this requires a long-term investment and, in some circumstances such as fast-moving markets or those with already-dominant players, may be a poor choice. In the time it takes to start a new company, the market may have passed you by. A faster way to get into a new business is to acquire another company that is already in that business.

Growth by acquisition is attractive because you get a going concern, usually staffed with experienced employees and already equipped with technology, trademarks, or other valuable assets. Buying a going concern is expensive, however, because you pay the owner for his effort and money invested in building the business to this point. If

the business is a fast-growing one, you may have to pay a premium for expected growth that is years away.

The big risk of acquisition is that you may not be buying what you think. Profits may not be as high as they look, due to short-term efforts by the seller to pump them up. The company's future prospects may also be poorer than you think, due to the vagaries of predicted market trends. It's not uncommon for acquirers to pay high prices to buy in at the peak of interest in a product or service, then watch profits shrink and market share dwindle under the pressure of competition or changing tastes. It happens even to sophisticated buyers. Quaker Oats bought Snapple for $1.7 billion only to sell the juice and iced-tea maker after three years for $300 million.

A Growth Perspective

Growth isn't for everybody. Some business owners never get the chance to grow. Others never have the inclination. But the same could be said of starting a business in the first place. If you love the excitement, challenge, and rewards of being an entrepreneur, you'll find them continually renewed as the owner of your own, growing company.

Where to Learn More

- *Growing Your Own Business* by Gregory and Patricia Kishel, published by Perigee, 1994. The Kishels, a husband-and-wife writing and small business management consulting team, cover in straightforward factual style the many details involved in expanding a business you've started.

- *Creating a Flexible Workplace: How to Select and Manage Alternative Work Options,* 2nd Edition by Barney Olmsted and Suzanne Smith, published by Amacom, 1994. A definitive guide to creative methods for balancing your business's people and productivity through the use of telecommuting, flextime, compressed workweeks, work sharing, and part-timers.

- *Gambling on Growth: How to Manage the Small High-Tech Firm* by S.T.P. Slatter, published by John Wiley & Sons, 1992. Although aimed at high-tech firms and containing some Eurocentric advice from its London Business School author, this is an insightful look at issues connected with small-business growth.

- International Franchise Association, 1350 New York Ave. NW, Suite 900, Washington, DC 20005, (202) 628-8000. This group provides many services and resources to prospective franchisers. Its *Franchise Opportunities Guide* is a $15 reference to approximately 300 franchise companies and includes answers to the most frequently asked questions about franchising.

ONLINE *small* business RESOURCES

The online world is rich with resources for the small business owner and person planning to start a business. Whether you subscribe to major online services such as America Online or CompuServe, or have Internet access through another service provider, you can find reams of statistics, research, guidebooks, and more to help you on your way.

Much of the information is available free, from government sources or commercial providers who want to attract small business people to their sites. You can even download free or low-cost software from many of the sites to help you plan and operate your business. And the beauty of the small business resources on the Internet is that they're available anytime, from anywhere a phone and computer will operate.

Small Business Administration

If you're only going one place online, this ought to be it. The SBA's Web site (http://www.sba.gov) and related resources may not make the zippiest reading, but its combination of scope and authority make it hands down the best place to get online help with starting a business.

The SBA information is, for the most part, free. But the main reason to love the SBA Web site is that it has almost everything you'll need. The first option when you reach the main page is to go to a section called "Starting Your Business." Other main sections include financing and expanding existing businesses.

Behind the categories are well-organized, concisely expressed manuals, tipsheets, and guides to many aspects of the topic. In "Starting Your Business," you can check out the "31 Most Asked Business Questions" or see the best business tips submitted by the small business owners selected as America's best.

Forget your fear of government-speak or bureaucratese. When you access one of these files you get plain, to-the-point tips. "How to Start a Small Business" begins by saying, "Starting and managing a business takes motivation, desire, and talent. It also takes research and planning." In what amounts to just a few double-spaced, typed pages of text, this section uses similar unadorned language to lead you to plumb your motivations as an entrepreneur and to rough out a business plan.

To help with your planning in more detail, there's a "Developing Your Business Plan Workshop." A section offering downloadable shareware programs for businesses includes many business planning templates for popular spreadsheet programs, as well as financial calculators, time management programs, and more.

What you don't find at the SBA Web site you are likely to locate at one of the many links accessible with a click or two. There's a link to the Service Corps of Retired Executives (SCORE), as well as to information on SBA-sponsored small business development and investment centers.

Not to be missed are SBA's links to the many other government agencies that collect information of use to entrepreneurs. The Census Bureau and Labor Department, to

name just two, are robust lodes of information on all kinds of markets, opportunities, and trends.

America Online

There is a lot for businessowners on the largest online service as well. Just type in the keyword "small business" to go straight to AOL's Your Business page.

You'll find a widely varied although somewhat disorganized mass of information here. Clicking one button from the Your Business page takes you to AOL's Business Travel Center, for instance, where you can go to research and plan to make the most of your road time. There are also alerts to online events such as AOL's Business Lunch, where small business owners gather to chat online to exchanges messages about issues and answers.

Other buttons lead you to an online store for products and services designed to appeal to small business owners: Business Newsstand with current information on business topics and Regional Resources, where AOL provides contact info for state and local small business organizations and agencies.

The meat of Your Business is in its six main subsections. Each has several levels of organization. Clicking on the section called The Dream, for instance, takes you to a page with links to resources specifically for start-ups. From The Dream you can click to a special section on start-up help, a small-business library, and links to the sites for Success Magazine and Entrepreneur Magazine on AOL.

The other main sections of Your Business are Getting Started, Finance Center, Sales & Marketing, Working the Web, and Tools & References. Sales & Marketing carries direct links to resources ranging from Guerrilla Marketing Online to AOL's own classified ads. One of the standout links is in Tools and References, where you can click to access a Business Owner's Toolkit of tutorials for starting, staffing, managing, or growing a business.

Entrepreneur Magazine Online

Entrepreneur Magazine's Web site (http://www.entrepreneurmag.com/) is actually the online home of several small business publications, including Business Start-Ups, Entrepreneur International, and the same publisher's new magazine on home-based businesses. It includes a broad and deep array of articles selected from those magazines. The result covers the waterfront on starting a business.

Franchising is an area of special emphasis. You can search a database of Entrepreneur's Franchise 500 as well as check out the 100 fastest growing franchises and the 150 lowest-cost franchises.

More general start-up help is available from the Small Business Library, Guide to Raising Money, and online information from Entrepreneur Magazine's Guide to Starting Smart. The Starting Smart guide, for instance, consists of ten articles excerpted from Business Start-Ups that take you from choosing your business concept through promoting your business. The material, though somewhat less authoritative than the SBA's, is rich in anecdotes and livelier than other Web sources.

Information flows both ways at the Entrepreneur site. You can send letters to the editors of the various publications, as well as exchange messages with other entrepreneurs and experts through several chat boards and forums. Special interest boards cover topics such as marketing, franchising, home-based business, and international trade.

Smart Business Supersite

The Smart Business Supersite (http://www.smartbiz.com/) was one of the first Web sites set up specifically to provide how-to information for small business owners, and it is one of the best. There are thousands of articles, hundreds of detailed product profiles, special services, online events, and vendors for any service you're likely to need.

SBS is a free site, with the cost of collecting and supplying the information provided by advertisers and vendors. And, since it minimizes the use of time-wasting graphics, you can find and get what you're looking for more quickly than on fancier sites.

There are scores of categories of information, from associations to worksheets. Many offer practical, authoritative advice or tools you can use immediately. For instance, one of the articles under Franchising is a detailed checklist for evaluating your suitability as a franchisee or small business buyer, excerpted from *The Franchise Bible,* by Erwin J. Keup, published by Oasis Press, 1995. SBS has an especially rich trove of more than 2,000 reviews of books, tapes, software, seminars, and publications for business-owners. You can often scan a reviewed magazine's table of contents, or get a sample newsletter issue online.

Business On the Net is a special section about making money online. It includes free articles, checklists, reports, and worksheets you can download or print out. There's also information about entrepreneurs' mailing lists you can sign up for, newsgroups to monitor, and other Web sites to visit for information and assistance with doing business on the Internet.

MetLife

You wouldn't think of an insurance company as a place to look for information on starting a business. But the Life Advice section of Metropolitan Life's Web site (http://www.metlife.com/Lifeadvi/Brochures/Startbiz/Docs/intro.html) is actually a trove of focused, basic tips on getting started in business.

The site's strength is its straightforward, rigorous organization. It leads you through the steps of starting a business. The first stop is a nine-question quiz to help you determine whether you have entrepreneurial personality traits.

Pass or fail, your next stop is a section on Getting Started, which helps you craft a business plan and has a scattering of tips on getting an accountant, advertising agency, and the like. Then comes Raising Money, Selecting a Legal Form, and more.

MetLife's information was developed in concert with the SBA and, therefore, is authoritative while echoing much of the advice contained in the SBA's own online resource. There are also some special offers for discounts on business guidebooks and a short listing of other resources such as newsgroups, organizations, and government Web sites.

The sophistication level of the MetLife Starting A Business site is basic. But if you're just getting started—and don't mind seeing Charlie Brown, Snoopy, or one of their pals on each page—MetLife's site is worth a trip.

Yahoo!

Yahoo! is a directory to all kinds of information on the Web, including excellent listings of information resources, sites, and organizations for small business owners. Yahoo! also maintains a directory of other directories and search engines to help you identify and tap into the Internet's vast resources on starting and staying in business. Go directly to http://www.yahoo.com/Business_and_Economy/Small_Business_ Information/ to begin your business search.

While it provides pointers to help, rather than actual advice on starting and running a business, Yahoo!'s listings often include brief descriptions of sites that help you decide where to look. For instance, its directory page of small business organizations includes First American Group Purchasing Association (http://www.firstgpa.com) and notes that it "provides purchasing and information resources and savings for small businesses through a network of suppliers." Yahoo! is fast, comprehensive, and friendly. It was the first Web directory and in some ways is still the best. Its limitation is that it searches only the information in its own directories. So if the Web site containing your information isn't already in Yahoo!, it might as well not exist.

Lycos

Lycos, at http://www.lycos.com, is another directory you can try. It's operated by Carnegie-Mellon University and is, if anything, even more comprehensive than Yahoo!. Lycos also maintains a directory of other directories and search engines to help you identify and tap into the Internet's vast resources on starting and staying in business.

THAT'S a WRAP!

By now you have more than a clue about what it would be like to start your own business. You know that there's most likely a way to independently, creatively, and productively fulfill your dreams of business ownership.

But you also know there's more to being in business than having an itch to be your own boss. You have to have the right personality. Your skills and experience have to fit the business you hope to start. You've got to think through a myriad of details, from how to structure your business and where to locate it to how to raise start-up money and market it.

Even after you've done it, you won't think going into business for yourself is easy. Through it all, you've got to balance often-competing interests.

While marketing for all your worth, for instance, you've got to keep a careful eye on quality. While selling as much as you can, you have to always ensure you're making a profit. While relying on your past experience, you've always got to be learning from other business people, experts, books, and even the World Wide Web.

The toughest balancing act, referred to over and over in this book, is the one between general advice and specific reality. Your business is unique. No other will face exactly the same combination of opportunity and obstacle. No other is intended to fulfill your ambition and your ambition alone.

Given that, there is no all-purpose advice that works for every business. But if there were, it would probably say: Plan carefully, and trust your instincts.

Planning

Planning is basic to business practice. Without planning, you're liable to miss opportunities and make mistakes. With it, you'll be in the position to make the most of opportunities and avoid errors.

Your business plan is your first line of defense against avoidable error and missed opportunity. Whether it's a 100-page model of perfection or a few notes scribbled on the back of an envelope, keep it handy.

Refer to your plan regularly. Once a month, once a quarter, or once a year would be suitable intervals. Checking your written assessment of your business's goals, methods, and resources will help keep you on track, make the most of effort you've already expended, and warn you against upcoming obstacles.

But don't be a slave to your plan. Events change. Goals change. Make sure your plan changes as well. Update it regularly and as events require.

Trust Your Gut

As you plan and start your business, you'll be consulting with advisers such as attorneys and accountants. You'll also be doing plenty of more or less structured analysis in the form of budgets, income statements, balance sheets, and cash flow forecasts.

Always pay attention to the experts. But remember: You're the entrepreneur. You're the one taking the most risk. No one else can tell you what to do. Many successful businesses have been founded on little more than the entrepreneur's insistence that it would work.

And never stop believing in the most important asset you and your business will ever have: Yourself.

GLOSSARY

accounts payable: Money that a company owes.

accounts receivable: Money that is due to a company from the sale of goods or services.

annual report: A document that includes detailed financial information and is presented to stockholders of a corporation once a year.

asset: Something of value. Money in the bank, receivables, inventory, fixtures, and equipment are examples of assets.

asset-based loan: A loan secured by the value of an asset.

balance sheet: A document that outlines a company's assets, liabilities, and equity of the owner at a particular point in time.

bankruptcy: The condition in which companies or individuals legally declare they are unable to pay their debts.

barrier to entry: A strategy that prevents one's competitors from offering the same product.

Big Six: The six largest accounting firms in the United States: Arthur Andersen, Ernst & Young, Deloitte & Touche, KPMG Peat Marwick, Price Waterhouse, Coopers & Lybrand.

board of directors: Managers elected by stockholders to oversee the daily operations of a corporation.

bond: A debt instrument issued by a company to raise money.

business plan: A document that outlines a company's goals, defines its product and market, provides financial data and résumés of key personnel, and serves as an operating tool to manage the business and obtain financing.

capitalization: The amount of money used to start a business.

cash flow: A measurement of a company's inflow and outflow of cash over a period of time.

Certified Public Accountant (CPA): An accountant who has met state requirements and has passed a series of exams.

chamber of commerce: An association of businesspeople that works to promote business in their geographic area.

Chapter 7: A form of bankruptcy in which a company sells its assets in order to pay its debts.

Chapter 11: A form of bankruptcy that allows a company to reorganize in order to meet its financial obligations and then resume operations.

collateral: Something of value used to guarantee a loan. If the borrower defaults, the creditor keeps the item that was pledged as collateral.

corporation: A business structure that sets up a company as a separate legal entity from its owners and enables it to raise capital through the sale of stock.

creditor: Someone to whom one owes money.

debt financing: A method of raising money for a business through loans or the sale of bonds.

default: Failure to pay a debt.

demographics: The characteristics of a population that marketers can use to determine which consumers would be most interested in their merchandise.

direct marketing: A strategy that consists of targeting a group of consumers who have a need for the products or services of a business, and mailing promotional materials to them.

disclosure statement: The document required by the Securities and Exchange Commission (SEC) at the time of a company's initial public offering (IPO) that states the purpose of the business, the number of shares of stock that will be offered, and what the company plans to do with the money it obtains from the sale of stock.

distribution: The process of transporting goods from the factory to the consumer.

dividend: A payment to owners of stock in a corporation.

earnings: A company's income.

economic development agencies: State and local government-operated departments that offer tax and other incentives, sponsor business incubation programs, and relax zoning regulations to encourage businesses to relocate or establish themselves in the area.

80/20 rule: The belief that 80 percent of a company's business comes from 20 percent of its customers.

equity: The value of stock.

equity financing: A method of raising money for a business through the sale of stock in exchange for partial ownership of the business.

estimated tax: An amount of tax calculated and prepaid on a quarterly basis.

factoring: A method of financing whereby a lender purchases the accounts receivables of a business at a discount to their face value.

fixed costs: A company's expenses that do not change regardless of the sales volume. Examples are rent, utilities, interest, and insurance premiums.

floor planning: A method of financing inventory whereby the lender bases the loan on the credit of the vendor as well as the credit of the business applying for the loan.

franchise: A business that is licensed by a larger company and operates under the regulations of that parent company. McDonald's is an example of a franchise.

freelancer: A person who works independently without commitment to any one company.

general partner: The partner in a limited partnership who has responsibility for the day-to-day management of the company.

going public: The process by which a company sells stock to the public.

guarantor: An individual who agrees to be responsible for the debts of another individual or business.

holding company: A company whose purpose is to hold stock in another company.

income statement: A document that outlines expenses, revenues, and net income of a business. Also known as a profit and loss (P & L) statement.

incorporate: To register a business with the state in order to separate its legal responsibilities from that of its owners.

initial public offering (IPO): The first time a stock is offered for sale to the public.

intangible asset: Something of value that has no physical properties. Examples are customer loyalty, goodwill, reputation, and trademarks.

interest: Payment for borrowing money.

inventory: Raw materials and finished products a company holds.

inventory turnover: The rate at which a company's inventory is sold out over a period of time.

investor: Someone who provides money in exchange for partial ownership of a company.

joint venture: Business structure that consists of two or more groups of people.

liability: An obligation to pay an amount to someone else.

limited liability corporation (LLC): Business structure that is taxed like a partnership and provides limited liability for its owners.

limited partnership: Business structure that consists of a general manager responsible for daily management decisions and who assumes liability for the debts, and investors who have little involvement and whose liability is limited to the amount of their investment.

line of credit: A type of revolving loan that lets a business borrow money as needed up to a set amount without having to reapply each time.

liquidate: To sell assets in order to raise cash.

liquidity: The ability of an asset to be converted to cash.

majority shareholder: Someone who owns at least 51 percent of the stock in a company.

markup: The difference between what it costs to produce an item and its selling price.

MBA: An advanced degree in business administration.

Nasdaq: An electronic stock market operated and regulated by the National Association of Securities Dealers (NASD), an organization of brokers and dealers.

net income: Total income less taxes and expenses.

net worth: The difference between the assets and liabilities of a company.

newsgroup: A feature of the Internet that allows participants to post messages and respond to each other.

New York Stock Exchange (NYSE): The largest and most active stock market in the world.

niche: A narrow segment of a market.

nonprofit organization: Business structure whose chief advantage is its exemption from paying taxes. The main disadvantage is that it is subject to a strict set of regulations. Designed generally for religious organizations, educational institutions, and social welfare organizations.

overhead: Expenses incurred as part of doing business. Examples are rent, utilities, and insurance.

over-the-counter (OTC): A method of selling securities electronically or by phone rather than at a stock market.

partnership: Business owned by two or more people who are jointly liable for the debts and assets of the company.

patent: A legal protection for a new product that prevents it from being copied for 17 years after its introduction.

point-of-purchase promotion: Marketing materials (brochures, posters, and the like) that are placed directly in a retail establishment.

positioning: A marketing strategy that defines a company or a product.

press release: A brief written message sent to reporters, editors, producers, and other members of the media that describes something newsworthy about a company or individual, the objective of which is to gain media exposure.

prime rate: A rate of interest to which other rates are pegged.

principal: The original amount of money borrowed or invested.

private placement: Sale of stock directly to specific investors rather than through a public offering.

privately held corporation: A company that does not issue stock to the public.

professional corporation: Business structure designed primarily for doctors, lawyers, and other professionals.

profit: Income after expenses have been deducted.

profit and loss (P & L) statement: [See: income statement.]

profit margin: The difference between a product's selling price and the cost of producing it.

promotion: Marketing strategies that use ads, newsletters, brochures, sweepstakes, and similar tools to transmit a message to prospective customers.

public relations: A form of marketing designed to increase a company's exposure in the media or community.

publicly held corporation: A company that issues stock for sale to the general public.

quarter: A period of three months.

research and development (R & D): The process of improving products or creating new ones and introducing them to the market.

revenue: A company's net income derived from the sale of its products or services.

Securities and Exchange Commission (SEC): A U.S. government agency that regulates the securities markets.

seed money: Start-up capital.

Service Corps of Retired Executives (SCORE): A division of the SBA that matches volunteer retired executives with entrepreneurs to provide confidential counseling, workshops, and training programs.

share: One unit of stock.

shareholder: An individual who owns stock in a company.

silent partner: An individual who invests in a company but does not take a role in running it.

Small Business Administration (SBA): An independent agency of the U.S. government that counsels, assists, provides financing for, and protects the interests of small businesses.

Small Business Development Centers (SBDCs): A network of information and guidance services administered by the SBA that provides free management and technical support to entrepreneurs through paid staff members and volunteers.

Small Business Institutes (SBIs): A division of the SBA, the SBI program provides counseling to small business owners by graduate level students and faculty.

Small Business Investment Companies (SBICs): Privately owned and managed investment firms, licensed and regulated by the SBA, that provide start-up and venture capital.

Small Company Offering Registration (SCOR): A quick and relatively inexpensive way to register stock for companies with assets under $3 million and less than 500 individual stockholders, which is available in 38 states.

sole proprietorship: Business structure in which one person owns and manages a company. Its advantages are that it is simple to set up and the owner maintains complete control and keeps all the profits. The disadvantages are that the owner assumes liability for all debts incurred, and the personal assets of the owner are at risk in the event of bankruptcy.

start-up: A new business.

stock: A share of ownership in a company.

Subchapter S corporation: A business structure of multiple owners that provides liability protection like a corporation does, but is taxed like a partnership.

supply and demand: The law of economics that states if there is a short supply of a commodity, the demand for it will cause its price to rise.

telemarketing: A strategy that uses the telephone to sell the products or services of a business.

tombstone: An advertisement that announces an initial public offering (IPO).

venture capital: Money provided by a pool of investors, to be used for starting or expanding a business, in exchange for partial ownership of the business.

RESOURCES

Books

Borrowing to Build Your Business. George M. Dawson (Upstart, 1997).

The Business Planning Guide, 7th Edition. David H. Bangs Jr.
   (Upstart, 1995).

The Entrepreneur Magazine Small Business Advisor. (John Wiley & Sons,
   1995).

Guerrilla Financing: Alternative Techniques to Finance Any Small Business.
   Bruce Blechman and Jay Conrad Levinson (Houghton Mifflin, 1992).

Guerrilla Marketing for the Home-Based Business. Jay Conrad Levinson and
   Seth Godin (Houghton Mifflin, 1995).

The Guerrilla Marketing Handbook. Jay Conrad Levinson and Seth Godin
   (Houghton Mifflin, 1995).

How to Buy a Great Business with No Cash Down. Arnold S. Goldstein (John
   Wiley & Sons, 1991).

How to Form Your Own Corporation without a Lawyer for Under $75.00. Ted Nicholas (Upstart, 1996).

How to Incorporate: A Handbook for Entrepreneurs and Professionals. Michael Diamond and Julie Williams (John Wiley & Sons, 1996).

How to Start, Finance, and Manage Your Own Small Business. Joseph R. Mancuso (Fireside, 1992).

Insuring Your Business: What You Need to Know to Get the Best Insurance Coverage for Your Business. Sean Mooney (Insurance Information Institute, 1993).

Legal Guide for Starting & Running a Small Business. Fred S. Steingold (Nolo Press, 1995).

Mancuso's Small Business Resource Guide. Joseph R. Mancuso (Sourcebooks, 1996).

101 Best Retirement Businesses. Lisa Rogak and David Bangs Jr. (Upstart, 1994).

Owning Your Own Franchise. Herbert Rust (Prentice Hall, 1991).

Positioning: The Battle for Your Mind. Al Ries and Jack Trout (Warner Books, 1993).

SBA Loans: A Step-by-Step Guide. Patrick D. O'Hara (John Wiley & Sons, 1994).

The Small Business Start-Up Guide. Hal Root and Steve Koenig (Sourcebooks Trade, 1994).

The Market Planning Guide. David H. Bangs, Jr. (Upstart, 1994).

Succeeding in Small Business: The 101 Toughest Problems and How to Solve Them. Jane Applegate (Plume, 1994).

Successful Telemarketing. Bob Stone and John Wyman (NTC Publishing, 1993).

Tax Savvy for Small Business: Year-Round Tax Advice for Small Business. Frederick W. Daily (Nolo Press, 1997).

The Upstart Small Business Legal Guide. Robert Friedman (Upstart, 1998).

The Under 35 Guide to Starting and Running a Business. Lisa Shaw (Upstart, 1996).

Working from Home: Everything You Need to Know about Living and Working under the Same Roof. Paul Edwards and Sarah Edwards (Putnam Publishing Group, 1994).

Magazines, Newspapers, and Other Publications

Business Week. 1221 Avenue of the Americas, New York, NY 10020, (800) 635-1200, $49.95/yr. (weekly).

Entrepreneur. P.O. Box 50368, Boulder, CO 80321, (800) 274-6229, $19.97/yr. (monthly).

The Family Business Advisor. P.O. Box 4356, Marietta, GA 30061, (770) 425-6673, $139/yr. (monthly).

Family Business Magazine. 1845 Walnut St., Ninth Floor, Philadelphia, PA 19103, (215) 567-3200, $95/yr. (quarterly).

Forbes. 60 Fifth Ave., New York, NY 10011, (800) 888-9896, $57/yr. (biweekly).

Fortune. P.O. Box 60001, Tampa, FL 33660, (800) 621-8000, $57/yr. (biweekly).

Home Office Computing. P.O. Box 53561, Boulder, CO 80322, (800) 678-0118, $19.97/yr. (monthly).

Inc. P.O. Box 54129, Boulder, CO 80332, (800) 234-0999, $19/yr. (18 issues).

Nation's Business. U.S. Chamber of Commerce Center for Small Business, 1615 H St. NW, Washington, DC 20062, (202) 463-5503, $22/yr. (monthly).

The New York Times. 229 West 43rd St., New York, NY 10036, (800) 631-2500, $374.40/yr. (daily).

Small Business Bulletin. Small Business Service Bureau, 554 Main St., Worcester, MA 01608, (508) 756-3513, free to members (6 times/yr).

The Wall Street Journal. 200 Liberty St., New York, NY 10281, (800) 568-7625, $175.00/yr. (daily).

Online Resources

American Express Web site, http://www.americanexpress.com/

America's Business Funding Directory. Matches businesses searching for capital with lending institutions or investors. Includes a guide designed to increase your chances of getting funding, information about small business centers and venture capital clubs, and a 30-day online classified ad service. http://www.businessfinance.com/search.htm

Business Filings Incorporated. For low-cost, online incorporating and formation of limited liability companies, and trademark search and registration services. http://www.bizfilings.com/incinfo.htm

BusinessWeek Online Web site, http://www.businessweek.com

Entrepreneur Magazine Online Web site, http://www.entrepreneurmag.com

Entrepreneurial Research Consortium (ERC). Information about a study conducted by Reynolds Entrepreneurial Research Consortium—a cooperative effort of almost 100 small-business researchers from 20 institutions—that examines start-ups and how they grow. http://www.babson.edu/entrep/res.html#erc2

Home Office Computing Online. America Online Keywords: HOC, SoHo

Inc. Magazine Online. America Online Keyword: Inc.

Internal Revenue Service Business Taxpayer Info Web site, http://www.irs.ustreas.gov/plain/search/site_tree.html

SBA Online Web site, http://www.sba.gov

The Small Business Advisor. For online advice on starting and running a small business. Includes information on business insurance, taxes, books, and U.S. government procurement, as well as links to other business-related sites. http://www.isquare.com/

The Small Business Resource Center. For free reports on choosing, starting, and running a small business; a catalog of books, tapes, and courses; and links to other small business resources. http://www.webcom.com/seaquest/sbrc/welcome.html

U.S. Business Advisor. Provides businesses with access to federal government information and services, including step-by-step guides, tools, answers to common questions, regulations, news, and links to other online resources. http://www.business.gov/index.html

U.S. Chamber of Commerce Center for Small Business Web site, http://www.uschamber.org

Venture Capital World on the Internet. For a direct database link between investors searching for opportunities and entrepreneurs looking for venture capital. http://www.vcworld.com

VirtualBusiness.Net. For frequently updated small business information, resources, and services, including VirtualBusiness.News, a weekly electronic newsletter with how-to's and feature articles; discussion forum; library with access to articles on business; and links to other online business resources. http://www.virtualbusiness.net/index.html#4

Associations and Organizations

American Association of Advertising Agencies (AAAA). 405 Lexington Ave., 18th Floor, New York, NY 10174, (212) 682-2500.

American Bankers Association. 1120 Connecticut Ave. NW, Washington, DC 20036, (202) 663-5000.

American Management Association (AMA). 1601 Broadway, New York, NY 10019, (212) 586-8100.

Bankers Systems. P.O. Box 1457, St. Cloud, MN 56302, (320) 251-3060.

The Center for Family Business. P.O. Box 24219, Cleveland, OH 44124, (216) 442-0800.

Ewing Marion Kauffman Foundation. 4900 Oak St., Kansas City, MO 64112, (816) 932-1000.

Federal Trade Commission. Sixth and Pennsylvania Ave. NW, Washington, DC 20580, (202) 326-2222.

General Services Administration. 18th & F Street NW, Washington, DC 20405, (202) 501-1231.

Independent Bankers Association. P.O. Box 267, 518 Lincoln Rd., Sauk Center, MN 56378, (320) 352-6546.

Independent Business Institute. 3234 South Cleveland-Massillon Rd., Norton, OH 44203, (330) 825-8258.

Institute of Management Consultants. 521 Fifth Ave., 35th floor, New York, NY 10175, (800) 221-2557.

National Association for the Self-Employed (NASE). P.O. Box 612067, DFW Airport, TX 75261, (800) 232-6273.

National Association of Home-Based Businesses. P.O. Box 362, 10451 Mill Run Circle, Suite 400, Owings Mills, MD 21117, (410) 363-3698.

National Association of Investment Companies (NAIC). 1111 14th St. NW, Suite 700, Washington, DC 20005, (202) 289-4336.

National Association of Small Business Investment Companies (NASBIC). 666 11th St. NW, Suite 750, Washington, DC 20001, (202) 628-5053.

National Association of State Development Agencies. 750 First St. NE, Suite 710, Washington, DC 20002, (202) 898-1302.

National Federation of Independent Business. Capitol Gallery East,   Suite 700, 600 Maryland Ave. SW, Washington, DC 20024, (202) 554-9000.

National Small Business United. 1156 15th St. NW, Suite 1100, Washington, DC 20005, (202) 293-8830.

National Venture Capital Association. 1655 North Fort Myer Dr., Suite 700, Arlington, VA 22209, (703) 351-5269.

The Open University. 24 South Orange Ave., Orlando, FL 32801, (407) 649-8488.

Procurement Automated Source System. Small Business Administration, 409 Third St. SW, Washington, DC 20416, (800) 231-7277.

Service Corps of Retired Executives (SCORE). Small Business Administration, 409 Third St. SW, Washington, DC 20416, (800) 827-5722.

Sheshunoff Information Services. One Texas Center, 505 Barton Springs Rd., Suite 1200, Austin, TX 78704, (512) 472-2244.

Small Business Administration. 409 Third St. SW, Washington, DC 20416, (800) 827-5722.

Small Business Legislative Council. 1156 15th St. NW, Suite 510, Washington, DC 20005, (202) 639-8500.

Small Business Service Bureau. 554 Main St., Worcester, MA 01608, (508) 756-3513.

U.S. Chamber of Commerce Center for Small Business. 1615 H St. NW, Washington, DC 20062, (202) 463-5503.

Veribank. P.O. Box 461, Wakefield, MA 01880, (617) 245-8370.

Business Forms Resources

The Complete Book of Small Business Legal Forms. Daniel Sitarz (Nova Publishing, 1996).

Court TV Small Business Law Center
http://www.courttv.com/legalhelp/business/

Small Business Administration Field Offices and Business Information Centers

Albany, NY	(518) 431-4261	Lewiston, ME	(207) 622-8242
Altanta, GA	(404) 347-4749	Los Angeles, CA	(213) 290-2832
Baltimore, MD	(410) 605-0990	Nashville, TN	(615) 749-4000
Boise, ID	(208) 334-9077	Newark, NJ	(201) 645-6049
Boston, MA	(617) 565-5615	Oklahoma City, OK	(405) 232-1968
Charleston, SC	(803) 853-3900	Omaha, NE	(402) 221-3606
Charlotte, NC	(704) 344-9797	Providence, RI	(401) 272-1083
Chicago, IL	(312) 353-1825	Randolph Center, VT	(802) 828-4422
Chiloquin, OR	(541) 783-2219	St. Louis, MO	(314) 539-6600
Chula Vista, CA	(619) 557-7250	Salem, OR	(503) 399-5181
Denver, CO	(303) 844-3986	Salt Lake City, UT	(801) 524-5804
El Paso, TX	(915) 534-0531	San Diego, CA	(619) 557-7252
Fairmont, WV	(304) 368-0023	Seattle, WA	(206) 553-5676
Ft. Worth, TX	(817) 871-6001	Spokane, WA	(509) 358-2050
Helena, MT	(406) 441-1081	Warm Springs, OR	(541) 553-3592
Honolulu, HI	(808) 522-8131	Washington, DC	(202) 606-4000
Houston, TX	(713) 773-6500	Wilmington, DE	(302) 831-1555
Kansas City, MO	(816) 374-6675		

SAMPLE BUSINESS PLANS

Yoyodyne Entertainment

Below is a sample executive summary, mission statement, and market analysis (description of business and industry) for a company that creates Internet games as marketing tools for its clients.

Executive Summary

The Internet is changing the nature of marketing. Advertisers have an entirely different set of tools at their disposal, and they're using new techniques to achieve extraordinary results.

Yoyodyne is the leader in Internet promotions and direct marketing, providing services for a wide variety of corporate clients. Using proprietary technology and compelling, fun games and contests, Yoyodyne has created custom and multisponsor promotions that have set new standards for effectiveness.

Yoyodyne's products deliver on a wide range of objectives, strategies, and tactics for our clients. From increasing brand awareness to building long-term, one-to-one relationships with a company's prospects and customers, Yoyodyne is able to utilize the frequency that only the Internet can deliver, and turn that frequency into effective marketing.

Last year, 58 percent of all advertising dollars were spent on direct mail and promotions. Yet few marketers have experience in bringing this type of measurable marketing to the Internet. Yoyodyne was one of the first to bring measurable marketing to the Internet and continues to push the envelope in creating groundbreaking online promotions and direct mail.

In the last year, Yoyodyne has given away the biggest cash prize in the history of the Internet, run the most popular interactive promotion of all time, and worked with over 100 clients, more than any other interactive promotions company.

Moving forward, Yoyodyne is investing in new technologies and new techniques to enable it to grab and hold the attention of an even larger base of people. With new affinity programs, consumer push, and more refined Web and e-mail promotions, Yoyodyne is positioned to continue its leadership role.

Mission Statement

Yoyodyne's mission statement is:

ENABLE RELATIONSHIPS BETWEEN CONSUMERS AND MARKETERS

Yoyodyne acts as a middleman, creating technologies and techniques that ENABLE marketers to develop relationships with consumers. In order to do this, Yoyodyne creates a compelling offer, communicates it in an arresting way, and then follows through with frequency and curriculum marketing. As the Internet becomes more crowded, Yoyodyne will continue to develop more interactive and memorable ways to reach out.

Yoyodyne defines a RELATIONSHIP as a two-part process. The first is permission. Permission to contact and to speak to the consumer. The second is frequency. Using the zero-incremental-cost efficiencies of the Internet, Yoyodyne can connect with people often enough to have a lasting impact.

BETWEEN consumers and marketers means just that. Yoyodyne does not rent or sell its player mailing lists to third parties.

CONSUMERS is defined quite broadly. A potential recruit for the KPMG accounting firm is a consumer from the point of view of the recruiter. Yoyodyne views the enabling technology as very democratic. Yoyodyne helps the marketer reach the audience needed in order to achieve its marketing objective.

MARKETERS are our clients. Almost without exception, Yoyodyne's best clients are those that understand the value (in specific monetary terms) of a new customer. Yoyodyne's goal is always to help the marketer add another new customer, or keep an old one, for less than the marketer could accomplish in any other medium.

The Market

The number of users of the Internet continues to grow. FIND/SVP estimates that 20 percent of U.S. households have Internet access and that over 50 million people use the Internet. These numbers are expected to double by the year 2000. Currently, almost all Internet users have an e-mail address while about half have access to the Web. Thus, e-mail is an important component in reaching the entire Internet user base. Just as important as reach is the frequency with which people use e-mail. Every study published has indicated that it is the number one use of the Internet. On America Online, the average user checks his e-mail daily.

Internet advertising has grown from $43 million in 1995 to an estimated $318 million in 1996, according to Jupiter Communications. As the Internet grows and as more companies integrate the Internet into their market strategies, the Internet advertising market is evolving from Internet-centric information technology companies to broader consumer industries. Internet advertising is expected to grow 71 percent annually, reaching $5 billion by the year 2000. Most of this advertising has been traditional broadcast- and magazine-type advertising. In the last six months, there has been a pronounced shift toward promotions and other measurable techniques.

Additionally, as more consumers access the Internet and become more comfortable with the medium, more of them will become electronic shoppers. Last year more than 2.5 million Web users bought $518 million worth of goods and services. A CommerceNet/Neilsen survey in March 1997 found that 53 percent of U.S. and Canadian Internet users used the Internet to reach a decision on a purchase, but that

15 percent carried out the transaction on the Web. Based on this survey, the Internet may have been used to reach a purchasing decision on over $3.5 billion of goods and services in 1996. Estimates vary widely on projections for Internet commerce in the year 2000, ranging from $6 billion to $60 billion.

As marketing and commerce online continue to develop, an ever-increasing percentage of funds and energies will be devoted to relationship-based activities. Yoyodyne, unique among its existing and emerging competitors, is premised on direct marketing concepts and the lifetime value of relationships. Yoyodyne is clearly well positioned to take advantage of the extraordinary advertising and promotional opportunities promised by the Internet and the Web.

Sales and Marketing Strategy

Yoyodyne's sales are primarily driven through its direct sale force. The sales and marketing team has developed a systematic approach for reaching clients directly or through their advertising agencies. Yoyodyne focuses not only on the companies that are spending advertising dollars on the Internet today, but also works to educate and develop long-term relationships with companies that will start spending dollars on the Internet tomorrow. Yoyodyne has had considerable public relations success (see Tab B) and has a significant market presence. Yoyodyne's other marketing efforts to advertisers include direct mail, advertising in trade publications, conventions, and its Internet presence. Yoyodyne continues to explore other sales strategies, including sales through third-party representative agencies.

The biggest hurdle for our sales force is the missionary work needed to bring new prospective clients into this arena. Yoyodyne is successful when a potential client has a budget and has a specific objective.

Yoyodyne has been very successful in bringing its promotions to potential consumer players and potential clients through its strategic deals with Netscape, Alta Vista, Geocities, and other well-known high-traffic sites on the Web.

Data Storage

Below is a sample summary, product description, and competition analysis for a company proposing to manufacture computer data storage devices.

Summary

This proposal summarizes all the pertinent information related to the establishment of a new business in the fastest expanding segment of the computer industry, namely, the I/O area. At no time has the market been as ready and accepting of such a venture as the present. Some of the highlights of this proposal are briefly summarized below:

The talent and experience of the founding group in the type of business to be pursued is superior to any in the industry.

The product is the fastest expanding segment of the computer industry.

The market in this type of equipment for OEM manufacturers is upwards of $80 million annually. Sales are expected to multiply rapidly, and we expect to become leaders in the high-performance tape drive business within five years.

With the advanced and highly reliable design that the founders will produce, it is a conservative estimate that this company will capture a minimum of 30 percent of this market within five years, which is $24 million.

Profitability is assured by the market requirements of this product, proven productivity and experiences of the founding group, and the low-cost manufacturing means that will be employed.

Product Line

Initial Product. The Company plans to pursue vigorously and at an accelerated pace the development, production, and marketing of two models of tape drives that are plug-to-plug compatible with the IBM 2420 line. These products will be superior to any other products on the market. Reliability will be built into the hardware by a simplified design, substituting electrical circuitry and pneumatics for mechanical mechanisms

whenever possible, reducing the number of adjustments, using the reliable phase encoding method of recording, and by offering automatic threading as a standard feature. Cartridge loading and NRZI capabilities will be offered on an optional basis.

Product Line

	DSD 2425	DSD 2427
Tape speed (ips)	100	200
Start time (ms)	3	2
Rewind time (sec)	72 (linear)	60 (linear)
Loading Method	Auto	Auto
Driving Method	Single capstan	Single capstan
Density (bpi)	1,600	1,600
Recording Method	Phase encoding	Phase encoding
Data rate (kb)	160	320
IBG (inches)	.6	.6
Tracks	9	9
Using Systems	360/30 and up	360/50 and up
	OEM	OEM

Features

Recording	NRZI	NRZI
Cartridge loading	Yes	Yes

Short-Term Product. In the second year of business and after the initial product is developed, the company will pursue the development of a lower speed drive and a controller.

Low-Speed Drive. This drive will move tape at 50 ips and will have all the reliability and set-up time improvements of the initial product. Design emphasis will be given to reducing cost without affecting reliability. This device will be aimed at small system users, i.e., 360/20 and 360/30, most of whom do not take advantage of the IBM 2420 line due to either unavailability or a low enough data rate or cost.

Controller. The controller will be designed to handle the company's drives and their IBM equivalent. It will be offered concurrently with the low-speed drive and will have the capability to control it. The addition of a controller to the product line will give the company flexibility in satisfying market demands. It will give us the ability to offer improvements in reliability and performance without having to hold them back due to the unavailability of a competitive controller that can handle them. For example, we will not be able to offer the lower speed drive on the schedule shown due to the unavailability of a competitive controller at that time.

Long-Term Products. For the long term, the company plans to extend its basic line both in speed and density of recording.

Also, a low-speed, low-cost line will be introduced. This line will consist of devices that generate 1/2-inch compatible tapes as well as noncompatible devices that use cassettes.

Competition

Computer manufacturers generally offer input-output devices with their systems. Most companies manufacture their own I/O equipment, including tape drives; others purchase them from OEM manufacturers. The most advanced tape drive subsystem

offered to date is the IBM 2420, which reestablished IBM as the leader in this field. Other computer manufacturers, such as Burroughs and Univac, usually buy their tape drives from OEM manufacturers. Honeywell and CDC, on the other hand, have been developing their own. None of the computer manufacturers have come up with a significant high-performance tape drive announcement recently, making it possible that they may purchase their future high-performance tape drive requirements from OEM sources.

In the OEM area, the key competitors are Potter, Telex, and Ampex. The first two have announced their intention to produce IBM 2420 compatible devices, and Potter has recently demonstrated an engineering model of a 200 ips drive.

The basic competitive strategy to be used by the company will consist of offering a superior product at a lower cost with a small price differential between the different models. The superiority of the initial product will be in the area of reliability and serviceability. Performance, on the other hand, will match that of the IBM 2420 to allow for plug-to-plug compatibility.

Our competitive position will be further enhanced by offering an IBM plug-to-plug compatible controller that will give us flexibility and freedom in offering performance and operational improvements. None of the OEM competitors offers controllers; therefore, they cannot offer improvements that are not consistent with what the computer manufacturers' controllers can handle.

To further gain early customer acceptance and satisfaction, a strong service organization will be established early and expanded as required.

A brief summary of the key OEM competitors is given below.

Potter. Potter Instrument was incorporated in 1942 as a manufacturer of counters and timers. The company now has a line of computer peripherals and a numerical control system for machine tools. The computer peripherals include printers, a random access tape loop device, and a range of tape drives for the military and OEM market. Potter's SC1080 tape drive is a single capstan IBM-compatible unit designed as a replacement for the IBM 729 and 2401 drives.

Potter's main facilities are situated in Plainview, Long Island, and consist of four plants with approximately 170,000 square feet of floor space. In addition Potter has 12,000 square feet of space in Puerto Rico. Yearly sales are over $30 million, with tape transports accounting for over 60 percent of their business.

Potter markets to OEM and through MAI. It markets the end user. The agreement with MAI retains the Washington, DC area for direct marketing to end users by Potter. The tie-in with MAI has had the effect of almost doubling Potter's tape drive sales during the past year.

Potter has announced and delivered 150 ips at 1,600 bpi phase encoded drives to Burroughs early this year. The company has also made known their intentions of building a 200 ips drive with automatic threading.

Technical support to system manufacturers is provided, but field service is the responsibility of the system manufacturer or the marketing organization. This is also the case with MAI, which leases and sells Potter drives to the end user.

Potter's main marketing strategy consists of lower prices, which generally run 1/3 less than IBM.

Laser Welding

Below is a sample product description, partial financials, and a marketing plan for a company selling laser welding equipment.

Products

LWD, Inc. will begin operation with a complete line of glass industrial lasers as well as a line of complimentary accessories. The pulsed glass laser line represents the latest technology in the field and is the end product of eleven years of intensive research at the American Laser Corp. This laser line will contain the following standard products:

1. Model 11—An industrialized laser system capable of performing both welding and drilling tasks at high production rates with minimal maintenance.

2. Model 14—Similar in design to the Model 11, but with twice the average power and the added advantage of a rectangular weld format.

3. Model 6—The Model 6 has been designed specifically for industrial drilling of small holes in a wide range of materials at production rates.

4. Model 103—Model 103 is a versatile laser welder/driller designed for research investigations as well as for those customers who desire to investigate a variety of potential applications prior to utilizing lasers on their production lines.

5. Microscope Laser—The microscope laser consists of a small laser integrated into a microscope. The unit is capable of producing spot sizes in the micron region and has been designed for the scientific and analytical laser markets.

6. Unilaser—A small, light-weight, low-cost laser system which has gained acceptance for a variety of uses in the educational, military, and scientific communities.

In addition to the laser line, the following line of accessories will also be marketed:

1. Laser protective eyewear and windows.

2. Laser safety sign and interlock package.

3. Optical delivery systems and components.

4. Alignment autocollimator.

Financials

Equity Positions. Albert Castro will put $15,000 cash into the company and will be a 60 percent owner of the business. William Lock will put $10,000 cash into the company and will be a 40 percent owner of the business. American Laser, Inc. has the option to receive either a 5 percent equity position in LWD, Inc. or a portion of after-tax profits for the years 1976 and 1977 as a partial payment to them for the business. No other equity positions are contemplated at this time.

Debt Financing. We have proposed to American Laser Corporation that they allow us to pay them $45,000 of the total we offer as a three-year note which would be senior to all other debt. In addition, a cash-flow analysis of our expected operation indicates a need for at least $50,000 additional cash. No other debt is contemplated at this time.

Operations (Expense/Sales) Sheet. To collect sufficient data and assumptions from which proforma cash-flows, a break-even analysis, and P&L Statements could be devised, a proforma operating sheet was made for the period June 18, 1973 to December 31, 1975. We believe, in general, that this sheet, shown in this section, is self-explanatory if we present the assumptions we made. Accordingly, they are:

Assumptions

1. American Laser, Inc. accepts our proposal as presented;

2. Outside funding group accepts our proposal as presented;

3. That our sales are as shown. That these sales estimates can be established by considering that:

> A) Torry Company will order two Model 11's for immediate delivery. Three more will be ordered within the first six months operation. We project six additional units in 1974, and up to eight more in 1975.

B) Foxboro Company will order one Model 14 within the first six months operation. We project one additional unit in 1974, and another in 1975.

C) Xerox will order a laser module within the first six months operation.

D) Past sales of accessories has been approximately $2,000 per month.

E) Applications work with Timex, Ethicon, Eastman Kodak, and Delco should result in some purchases in 1974 and 1975.

4. That no expenses other than those shown in the operations sheet be incurred.

Proforma Cash Flow. Using data from the Operations Sheet, a proforma cash flow analysis was made and is also given in this section. In making this projection of cash flow, it was assumed that all bills owed were paid within 30 days, all accounts receivable to us were paid within 30 days, and no cash payouts other than those shown were to be made.

Marketing Plan: First Six Months

Direct Selling. Direct selling will be accomplished during the first six months of operation via two manufacturers' rep firms retained from American Laser, Inc. as well as from a 75 percent selling effort from Bill Lock and 25 percent selling effort from Al Castro. The firm of Cook & Weil, Inc. will cover all of California and the firm of Robinson Associates will cover upper Oregon and Washington. The two rep firms will be paid on direct commission from sales in their respective areas. Al Castro and Bill Lock will concentrate on the Arizona area with the heaviest concentration in Phoenix. Bill Lock will spend as much time as required with the Torry Co., and the Foxboro Co.

Promotion. News releases will appear in the local newspapers as well as the appropriate technical publications announcing the formation of our business as well as our goals and products. Al Castro and Bill Lock will actively solicit speaking engagements to California engineering groups and business groups. These talks will strongly stress lasers as a machine tool showing advantages over existing techniques. In addition, speaking engagements at technical shows will be solicited.

Advertising. Accessories: An ad will appear in *Laser Focus* under our new company name during September featuring our safety accessory kit and autocollimator. A follow-up ad will appear in November.

Advertising. Laser Systems: We will place ads in "local" technical-business publications in the West Coast market areas. These will be supplemented by application news releases in the local press.

Applications. Robert Dusza will spend 75 percent of his time and Bill Lock 25 percent of his time actively performing studies on potential applications. Potential customers will be strongly urged to visit the plant and see the equipment in actual operation.

Assistance to Reps. We will provide our two rep firms with support via trips and communication with their potential customers as well as with all the necessary selling aids such as sample applications, literature, an accessory kit, and potential leads. Both Al Castro and Bill Lock will schedule trips into the reps' areas on a periodic basis. This will allow our reps to make maximum use of our time when we are in their areas.

Price. For this period of time, we would be selling off the already built inventory, be building back what we sell, and selling for 1974 sales. In this period, we will leave the price structure the same as it was under American Laser, Inc. management. The current gross margin on the Models 11, 14, 6, 103 is approximately 50 percent, but we should attain a greater per-unit contribution margin, in our small company, than could be achieved in the larger company.

Marketing Plan: Beyond Six Months

Direct Selling. A direct factory salesman will be added to our organization during March of 1974. The type of individual we will be looking for must have a strong technical background as well as proven sales ability in the area of industrial sales. We anticipate that he will spend his first months both training at the plant as well as visiting existing customers. He will operate on straight salary for his first three months. By June of 1974, he will be ready to go out into the field. His assignment at that time will be somewhat dependent on the effectiveness of our rep organization as well as our feelings toward further geographical expansion. Al Castro and Bill Lock will continue

to do some selling, but as time goes on, their time will be increasingly required on internal operations, and therefore a smaller percentage of their time will be available for direct selling.

Promotion. We believe that promotion is by far the most important factor of the marketing mix for our products. It is our plan that approximately 5 percent of sales be allocated to expenses for promotion. Bill Lock will be responsible for this activity and he plans to continue with speaking engagements, putting out news releases, writing a few technical articles for suitable trade publications, taking movies of our equipment satisfactorily performing to show potential customers in similar industries, etc.

Advertising. We do not plan to substantially change our expenditures for advertising during the first three years of operation. It is planned that the ads will be designed to reach a particular identified group for each particular product of our company. This will mean that our ads will be appearing in different publications, more direct mailing will result, as well as less "capability or image" advertising than was the case at American Optical.

Applications. Robert Dusza will spend 75 percent of his time, as before, doing applications work. Bill Lock will have more time to allot to applications (because of the addition of the direct salesman) and will continue to lead this all-important work in our operation.

Assistance to Reps. As in first six-month plan.

Price. We believe that our lasers and a few of our accessories could be priced 15 percent higher than they currently are and still remain competitive. We plan now to institute this increase in price early in 1974. As we will be strongly influenced in making this decision by our competition's prices at that time, our anticipated sales projections and cash flow calculations shown in the financial section of this proposal do not reflect this anticipated price increase.

Note: The Data Storage and Laser Welding business plans are reprinted with permission from The Center for Entrepreneurial Management.

INDEX